MW00635578

By Scripture Alone

BY THE SAME AUTHOR

*What Calvin Says: An Introduction to
the Theology of John Calvin*

The Scripturalism of Gordon H. Clark

A Study Guide to the Westminster Confession of Faith

By Scripture Alone

W. Gary Crampton

The Trinity Foundation

By Scripture Alone

Copyright © 2002 W. Gary Crampton
Published by The Trinity Foundation
Unicoi, Tennessee
http://www.trinityfoundation.org/

ISBN: 0-940931-59-1

Contents

This book is dedicated
to the memory of Dr. Gordon H. Clark
and to Dr. John W. Robbins:
Defenders of the faith once delivered to the saints.

Foreword

No DOCTRINE is of greater importance today, given the sad state of affairs within professing Christendom, than the Protestant doctrine of *sola Scriptura*. Realizing this, Dr. Gary Crampton argues the case anew within these pages for the Bible as the only infallible authority and guide in matters of faith and life. He does this in Part One by leading his readers, Section by Section, through the famous first chapter of the *Westminster Confession of Faith* titled "Of the Holy Scriptures," explicating the necessity, the "inspiredness," the self-validating authority, the sufficiency, the perspicuity, the preservation, the infallible self-interpreting character, and the finality of the Christian Scriptures. One does not have to agree with every sentence in Part One in order still to be moved afresh to praise God for the repleteness of the data of Scripture concerning these mighty attributes of God's Word to needy men and women.

Because Protestantism's view of Holy Scripture is diametrically opposed to the Roman Church-State view of Scripture and church authority at virtually every point, it is not surprising that the Roman Church-State has opposed the Protestant view of Scripture since the days of the Reformation to this very day. A recent volume opposing the Protestant doctrine of *sola Scriptura* is *Not by Scripture Alone: A Catholic Critique of the Protestant Doctrine of Sola Scriptura*, edited by Robert A. Sungenis. In Part Two of this book Dr. Crampton squarely faces, chapter by chapter, the contentions of the several Romanist apologists who argue that Scripture and Church Tradition are of equal importance and together compose the Church's authority in matters of faith and life, and he shows that the Sungenis volume is wanting at virtually every point. Again, one does not have to agree with every sentence in Part Two in order still to thank God for Dr. Crampton's careful analyses of the conclusions of the Sungenis volume.

Dr. Crampton's book shows that the fundamental epistemological issue of authority that divided Rome from Wittenberg and Geneva in the sixteenth century is still with us, and despite the change in Rome's public tone today with respect to the "separated brethren" of Protestantism, the issue of authority that divided Rome from the Reformation, has, if anything, actually been exacerbated by the papal claim to infallibility.

I am confident that Dr. Crampton's readers will find this work clear, fair, and accurate. I commend its close reading.

Robert L. Reymond
Fort Lauderdale, 2002

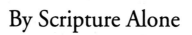

By Scripture Alone

Introduction

THE WESTMINSTER Assembly of divines (men who studied and taught "divinity" or theology) was summoned by an Act of Parliament to unite England, Scotland, and Ireland through the composition and adoption of a single creed. The Puritan Parliament formed the Assembly in 1643, and its multi-year consultation produced several documents, including the *Westminster Confession of Faith* (1647) and the *Larger* (1648) and *Shorter* (1648) *Catechisms*. Together these documents are referred to as the Westminster Standards. Although they were not adopted by Parliament, the Standards are still today the adopted standards of conservative Presbyterian churches as well as a number of other Reformed churches throughout the world. They are widely recognized as one of the finest systematic summaries of Holy Scripture ever produced in creedal form. In the words of the Princeton theologian B. B. Warfield, they are "the final crystallization of the elements of evangelical religion, after the conflicts of sixteen hundred years.... They are the richest and most precise and best guarded statement ever penned of all that enters into evangelical religion and of all that must be safeguarded if evangelical religion is to persist in the world."[1]

The original group of more than 140 theologians were Calvinistic in their theology. Presbyterianism was the dominant

1. Benjamin B. Warfield, *Selected Shorter Writings*, edited by John E. Meeter (Presbyterian and Reformed, 1973), II:660.

position on church government. These men met over a period of five years and six months in 1,163 sessions. They daily engaged in solid Biblical exegesis from the original languages. The Bible was absolutely foundational in the work of the divines. The primary rule these men laid down for themselves as they began their work was: "What any man undertakes to prove as necessary, he shall make good out of Scripture." Each Monday morning every member was required to take the following vow: "I do seriously promise and vow, in the presence of Almighty God, that in the Assembly whereof I am a member, I will maintain nothing in point of doctrine but what I believe to be most agreeable to the Word of God."[2]

Scripture, then, was the axiomatic starting point of the Assembly. Epistemology (the theory of knowledge) was the issue that first needed to be addressed, for it is the key component of any theological or philosophical system. Thus, the authors of the *Westminster Confession of Faith* did not begin with the doctrine of God; this was left to chapters 2 through 5. "God," as an axiom, apart from Scripture, is merely a proper name. What must be specified is "which God."[3] Therefore, chapter 1 has to do with our source of knowledge: "Of the Holy Scripture."

Metaphorically speaking, then, as Gordon Clark taught, the first chapter of the *Confession* stands as a "continental divide."[4] The Word of God, which has been the touchstone of pure doctrine throughout the centuries, forms a great divide between

2. John R. Richardson, "Introduction," to Gordon H. Clark, *What Do Presbyterians Believe?* (The Trinity Foundation [1965] 2001), xi-xiv.

3. This is the reason that the *Shorter Catechism* (Q. 4) does not ask the question "Is there a god," but "What is God?" The answer then identifies the God of Scripture: "God is a Spirit, infinite, eternal, and unchangeable, in His being, wisdom, power, holiness, justice, goodness, and truth."

4. Clark, *What Do Presbyterians Believe?* 275.

Christianity and all other types of thought. In "Of the Holy Scripture" the Westminster divines discuss (among other things) the necessity of Scripture, the identity of Scripture, the inspiration of Scripture, the authority of Scripture, the self-authentication of Scripture, the sufficiency of Scripture, the clarity of Scripture, the transmission and preservation of Scripture, the interpretation of Scripture, and the finality of Scripture, all of which are essential for a proper understanding of the Word of God. And it is because of these essential marks or attributes of the Bible that the Reformers held to the principle of *sola Scriptura*: Scripture alone has a systematic monopoly on truth; it is the sole criterion of truth. This is why the Preface of the 1611 King James Version described the Bible as "A Pandect [complete body] of Profitable Laws, against Rebellious Spirits."

To ignore, reject, or attack any one of these attributes is to ignore, reject, or attack the Word of God and the God of the Word. We are forbidden to add to or to take away from the written Word of God (*Deuteronomy* 4:2; *Proverbs* 30:6; *Revelation* 22:18-19). Yet, it is precisely at this point that opponents of Christianity – modernists, Pentecostal-Charismatics, Greek Orthodox and Roman Catholics – have made their most determined attacks on Christianity, that is, at the foundation. The most vehement opponent and enemy of God and the true church through the centuries has been the one the *Confession* (25:6) calls the Antichrist himself: "the pope of Rome," the Roman Church-State. "The Canons and Decrees of the Council of Trent" go so far as to anathematize anyone who adheres to the Reformed doctrine of *sola Scriptura*.[5] This is why William Whitaker wrote:

5. Fourth Session, April 8, 1546. See Philip Schaff, editor, *The Creeds of Christendom* (Baker Books, 1983), II:79-82.

"If ever any heresies have impiously outraged the Holy Scripture of God, we may justly rank the papists [Roman Catholics]...with this class of men, who pervert things most sacred."[6]

Dr. Archie Jones has pointed out that the Protestant Reformation, at its root, was a movement to replace the Roman Catholic standard of oral tradition (that has allegedly been passed down from Peter to the popes), which is considered equal to or even greater than Scripture (because the Roman Church-State considers itself to be the author and finisher of Scripture), with "a return to the Bible as the only infallible standard of faith and practice."[7]

A recent assault on the Word of God is a book titled *Not By Scripture Alone: A Catholic Critique of the Protestant Doctrine of Sola Scriptura*.[8] The authors of this book attempt to demonstrate that the Protestant doctrine of *sola Scriptura* is errant. And understandably they take aim at the teachings of the first chapter of the *Westminster Confession*, knowing that it is as clear a rendering of the Protestant doctrine as can be found in creedal form. If they are successful, of course, the rest of Reformed and Calvinistic thinking is obviated. The good news is that *Not By Scripture Alone* fails. Romanism's Aristotelian epistemology is a failure; thus, the whole of its system rests, as Christ taught, on sinking sand (*Matthew* 7:26-27).

Lorraine Boettner was correct when he wrote:

6. William Whitaker, *A Disputation on Holy Scripture* (University Press, 1610; republished by Still Waters Revival Books), 705.

7. Archie P. Jones, *The Influence of Historic Christianity on Early America* (Chalcedon Foundation, 1998), 22.

8. Robert A. Sungenis, *et al.*, *Not By Scripture Alone: A Catholic Critique of the Protestant Doctrine of Sola Scriptura* (Queenship, 1998).

[T]he Achilles heel of Romanism is the false theological basis on which the system rests…[and] the strength of evangelical Protestantism is its rigid adherence to what the Scriptures teach. Protestantism can never defeat Romanism, nor even defend itself against Romanism, merely by pointing out the latter's corrupt political alliances, its inordinate greed for money, and its suppression of political and religious liberties. All of these things are true and should be exposed. But they relate only to external methods and practices. Romanism is basically a religious system and must be challenged and forced to defend its doctrines on the basis of Scripture [alone]. This method, and this method alone, can bring victory to the evangelical faith.[9]

This book intends to show that the doctrine of Scripture taught by the Westminster Standards is the Biblical view:

The whole counsel of God concerning all things necessary for His own glory, man's salvation, faith, and life, is either expressly set down in Scripture, or by good and necessary consequence may be deduced from Scripture: unto which nothing at any time is to be added, whether by new revelations of the Spirit, or traditions of men.

Part One of this book is a commentary or analysis of chapter 1 of the *Westminster Confession of Faith:* "Of the Holy Scripture." Part Two is written as a response to *Not By Scripture Alone*, based on what is discussed in Part One.

9. Lorraine Boettner, *Roman Catholicism* (Presbyterian and Reformed [1962] 1986), 450.

Part One

The Westminster Assembly's Doctrine of Holy Scripture

Part One
The Westminster Assembly's Doctrine of Holy Scripture

B. Warfield wrote that "there is certainly in the whole mass of confessional literature no more nobly received or ably wrought-out statement of doctrine than the chapter 'Of the Holy Scripture,' which the Westminster divines placed at the head of their *Confession* and laid at the foundation of their system of doctrine."[1] Philip Schaff, certainly no Calvinist, commented that "No other Protestant symbol has such a clear, judicious, concise, and exhaustive statement of this fundamental article of Protestantism.... [It is] the best Protestant counterpart of the Roman Catholic doctrine of the rule of faith."[2]

By way of a broad outline of this monumental chapter we might say that Section 1 has to do with the necessity of Scripture; Sections 2 and 3 treat the identity or definition of Scripture; Sections 4 and 5 deal with the authority of Scripture; Section 6 asserts the sufficiency of Scripture; Section 7 teaches the clarity or perspicuity of Scripture; Section 8 is on the transmission and preservation of Scripture; Section 9 concerns the interpretation of Scripture; and Section 10 concludes the chapter

1. Benjamin B. Warfield, *The Westminster Assembly and Its Work* (Still Waters Revival Books, 1991), 155.
2. Philip Schaff, editor, *The Creeds of Christendom*, I:767.

focusing on the finality of Scripture. And, as we will see, the Roman Church-State, in one way or another, disavows all of these attributes or marks of Scripture, and in so doing reveals its system to be both false and Antichristian.

The Necessity of Scripture

1:1 Although the light of nature, and the works of creation and providence do so far manifest the goodness, wisdom, and power of God, as to leave men inexcusable; yet are they not sufficient to give that knowledge of God, and of His will, which is necessary unto salvation. Therefore it pleased the Lord, at sundry times, and in divers manners, to reveal Himself, and to declare His will unto His church; and afterward, for the better preserving and propagating of the truth, and for the more sure establishment and comfort of the church against the corruption of the flesh, and the malice of Satan and of the world, to commit the same wholly unto writing: which makes the Holy Scripture to be most necessary; those former ways of God's revealing His will unto His people being now ceased.

The Bible teaches that God has revealed Himself to mankind in both general and special revelation. General revelation is so called because it is general in audience (all mankind) and limited in content. Special revelation, on the other hand, which is now found only in the Scriptures, is more restricted in audience (those who hear or read the Bible), and much more detailed in content. Due to its limited nature, general revelation must always be interpreted in the light of special revelation. This was true before the fall of man (*Genesis* 3), but even more so afterward, because the universe, including man, is now in a state of abnormality (*Genesis* 3:14-19; *Romans* 8:19-25).

When the Westminster Assembly referred to "the light of nature," it spoke of that innate idea of God that God has implanted in all men. This was stated more fully by the *Confession* in a later chapter (21:1): "The light of nature shows that there is a God, Who has lordship and sovereignty over all, is good, and does good unto all, and is therefore to be feared, loved, praised, called upon, trusted in, and served, with all the heart, and with all the soul, and with all the might." The Apostle Paul teaches about this innate light in *Romans* 1:18-21, 32 and 2:14-15, pointing out that it does not come by means of sensory experience, and that it includes a sense of morality. Again, to cite the *Confession* (4:2): "After God had made all other creatures, He created man, male and female...after His own image, having the law of God written in their hearts." This light of nature, which John Calvin (1509-1564) spoke of as the *sensus deitatis*,[3] is both propositional and ineradicable. This is due to the fact that all men are created in the image of God (*Genesis* 1:26-28). Man's mind is not a *tabula rasa* (blank tablet) at conception or birth. As B. B. Warfield stated, for both Calvin and Augustine (354-430), this innate or *a priori* idea lies at the root of all man's information about God and His creation. This was especially true of Augustine. Warfield said that according to Augustine:

> In a word, the soul is [richly equipped] for the perception and understanding of the sensible world only by prior perception and understanding of the intelligible world. That is to say, the soul brings over from the intelligible world the forms of thought under which alone the sensible world can be received by it into a mental embrace.[4]

3. John Calvin, *Institutes of the Christian Religion*, John T. McNeill, editor, translated by Ford Lewis Battles (Westminster Press, 1960), I:3:1.
4. Benjamin B. Warfield, *Calvin and Augustine*, edited by Samuel G. Craig (Presbyterian and Reformed [1956] 1980), 394.

Because of these innate ideas God the Creator is perceived through His creation (*Romans* 1:18-21; *Psalm* 19:1-6). When man interacts with creation, which illustrates some of God's glory, power, and wisdom, man, as God's image, ineluctably "thinks God." It is not as though the visible creation itself mediates knowledge to man, as in the teaching of Thomas Aquinas (1225-1274), for the visible creation sets forth no propositions, and knowledge can come only by means of propositions, for only propositional statements can be true or false. Rather, as Augustine taught, it stimulates the mind of man to intellectual intuition or recollection, who as a rational being is already in possession of *a priori*, propositional information about God and His creation.[5]

General revelation, then, reveals God to all men and leaves all men without excuse (*Romans* 1:20). But due to the effects of sin on the mind, fallen man, even though he possesses this seed of true religion, continually suppresses the information he has and cannot avoid (*Romans* 1:20). Hence, as sufficient as general revelation is to reveal God to all men, leaving them inexcusable, it is insufficient, as the *Confession* says "to give that knowledge of God, and of His will, which is necessary unto salvation … which makes the Holy Scripture to be most necessary."

As clear as the Bible seems to be on this matter, the Roman Church-State disagrees. Romanism has long taught that those "who, through no fault of their own, do not know the Gospel of Christ or His church, but who nevertheless seek God with a sincere heart, and, moved by grace, try in their actions to do His

---

5. See Gordon H. Clark, "Augustine of Hippo," *The Encyclopedia of Christianity*, edited by Edwin H. Palmer (The National Foundation for Christian Education, 1964), I:485-493.

will as they know it through the dictates of their conscience – those too may achieve eternal salvation."[6] Or said another way, according to Rome, if man diligently seeks to do what is right according to the knowledge he has of God through general revelation, he "too may achieve eternal salvation." Against this universalist heresy, the *Confession* (10:4) teaches the Biblical view that "men not professing the Christian religion," cannot "be saved in any other way whatsoever, be they ever so diligent to frame their lives according to the light of nature." Without special revelation, that is, without the propositional truth of God's Word, then, sinful man is not able to come to a sound and saving knowledge of God. The necessity of special revelation rests on both the insufficiency of general revelation and the sinfulness of man.

Although the Bible does teach the doctrine of general or natural revelation, it does not teach a natural theology, that is, that it is possible for man to articulate true knowledge of God by means of general revelation alone (without the aid of special revelation). John Calvin, for example, taught that the innate sense of God, and the daily disclosure of God through creation, are more than adequate to show the God of Scripture to be the one and only true God. He spoke of the plausibility of the arguments for God's existence: the religious or moral argument, the cosmological argument, the argument from the common benevolence of God, and the argument from the human anatomy. But, said Calvin, unaided by the "spectacles" of special revelation, these all speak to us in vain.[7] Not even the knowledge of the resurrec-

---

6. *Lumen Gentium*, 16, as cited in Robert L. Reymond, *A New Systematic Theology of the Christian Faith* (Thomas Nelson Publishers, 1998), 1085n.
7. Calvin, *Institutes* I:1-6.

tion of Jesus Christ led the disciples to faith; it merely confirmed the faith they already possessed.[8] Calvin concluded: "The proofs of faith must be [sought at] the mouth of God *alone* [emphasis added]. If we dispute about matters which concern men, then let human reasons take place; but in the doctrine of faith, the authority of God alone must reign, and upon it we must depend."[9] One should not attempt to prove God; He is the necessary premise of all proof, the object of knowledge better known than any other.

Here again, however, Roman Catholicism demurs. Romanism teaches that the existence of God can indeed be proved on the basis of sensory observation and reason. First is the ontological argument, developed by Anselm (1033-1109), Archbishop of Canterbury, and restated by René Descartes (1596-1650).[10] And second, and most important, there are the arguments of the disciple of Aristotle, Thomas Aquinas (his "Five Ways").

According to Gordon Clark (1902-1985), basically the ontological argument asserts that "God, by definition, is the being Who possesses all perfections; existence is a perfection; therefore God exists."[11] There are several problems with this argument. First, it should be said that the syllogism as stated is formally valid. The trouble is not with the form of the argument, but with its terms. Existence, for example, is an attribute that applies to everything. Dreams exist; hallucinations exist; mi-

8. Calvin, *Institutes* II:2:2-5.

9. John Calvin, *Commentaries*, Volumes I-XXII (Baker Book House, 1981), *Commentary* on *Acts* 17:2.

10. See Gordon H. Clark, *Thales to Dewey* (The Trinity Foundation [1957] 2000), 202-208, 244-256.

11. Gordon H. Clark, *A Christian Philosophy of Education* (The Trinity Foundation [1946] 2000), 29.

rages exist. The question is not whether something exists; the question is, What is it that exists? This is precisely why the Westminster Assembly asked the question the way it is found in the *Shorter Catechism* (Q. 4): "What is God?" rather than "Is there a god?" The ontological argument is not an argument from something extra-Biblical to God. The definition of God found in the argument itself includes elements smuggled in from Scripture, including monotheism.

Second, Thomas Aquinas believed that he (or, rather, Aristotle) had constructed several demonstrations of God's existence in his famous "Five Ways": the argument from motion, the argument from efficient causality, the argument from contingent beings, the argument from the gradation of perfection, and the argument from design, all of which are arguments from effects to cause. By them, Aquinas attempted to demonstrate the existence of God from sense data. Thomas also believed that he could demonstrate the supernatural origin of the Roman Church-State, thereby establishing its authority and the truth of the revealed matters on which it speaks.[12]

Thomas' arguments are all invalid, for the following reasons: First, one cannot begin with sense data and proceed to deduce non-sensory conclusions, such as God. What is not at least implicitly in the premises of an argument cannot appear in the conclusion. Second, Aquinas averred that the universe as a whole is an effect, but no observation of the parts of the universe can give us this conclusion; and no one has observed the universe as

12. Thomas Aquinas, *Summa Theologiae*, I, 2-3, and *Summa contra Gentiles*, I, xiii. See also Clark, *Thales to Dewey*, 215-225; Norman L. Geisler, *Thomas Aquinas: An Evangelical Appraisal* (Baker Book House, 1991), 119-135; and Millard J. Erickson, *Christian Theology* (Baker Book House, 1983-1985), 157-158.

a whole (this is the fallacy of composition). Third, Aquinas taught that man's mind is a *tabula rasa* prior to sense impressions, but this view of the mind of man as a blank slate prior to sense experience is a logical absurdity. That is, a consciousness which is conscious of nothing is a contradiction in terms. Fourth, Thomas said that nothing could be predicated of God in the same sense that it could be predicated of a creature. Hence, when he argued from the existence of the world to the existence of God, he was using the term *existence* in two different senses; herein he committed the logical fallacy of equivocation. And finally, if the Five Ways of Aquinas could prove the existence of a god or gods, they would prove too much. That is, they would prove the falsity of the Bible. How could one know if the five proofs even prove the same god? Perhaps they prove that there are two, three, four, or five gods.[13]

We have seen in the Introduction that epistemology (the theory of knowledge) is the key component of any theological or philosophical system. All subject matter claiming to be intelligible or cognitive is controlled by some epistemology. A Christian epistemology is not founded upon rationalism or empiricism. Neither is the knowledge that man has of God and His creation in any sense mediated knowledge. Rather, all knowledge is immediate, revelational, and propositional. The "inward Teacher," Jesus Christ, the divine *Logos*, not the senses, teaches man (*Matthew* 23:8; *John* 1:9). This is true even with regard to the printed pages of the Bible. All speech or writing is a matter of words, and words are signs, in that they signify something. When signs are used, the recipient, in order to understand, must already know

13. Gordon Clark, *Thales to Dewey*, 217-221; Reymond, *A New Systematic Theology of the Christian Faith*, 135-136.

that which is signified. Apart from this knowledge, signs would be meaningless.[14]

The Bible is not to be thought of as black ink on white paper. God's Word is eternal; the printed pages of the Bible are not. The letters and words on the printed pages are signs or symbols which signify the eternal truth which is in the mind of God and which is communicated by God directly and immediately to the minds of men. A Christian epistemology has its roots in the *Logos* doctrine of the *Gospel of John*. According to the *Gospel of John*, Jesus Christ is the cosmological *Logos* (1:1-3), the epistemological *Logos* (1:9, 14), and the soteriological *Logos* (1:4, 12, 13; 14:6). He is the Creator of the world, the source of all human knowledge, and the giver of salvation. As to the epistemological *Logos*, which is the current focus, Christ is the "true light which enlightens every man" (1:9).[15]

Another way of explaining this is to say that a Biblical epistemology teaches that the sum of all truth exists in the mind of God. There is no truth outside of the mind of God. That is the meaning of "omniscient" and "omnipresent." Hence, if man is going to know the truth, he must come to know propositions in the mind of God. Scripture tells us that some of these propositional truths are implanted in man from conception by God. They constitute man as God's image. When man interacts with creation or reads the words of Scripture, the divine Teacher, the *Logos*, illuminates the mind so that the propositions come to explicit consciousness. This is possible because the mind of man is enveloped by the mind of the *Logos*, Who enlightens him to

14. Gordon H. Clark, *The Johannine Logos* (The Trinity Foundation [1972] 1989), chapter 2; Augustine, *On the Teacher*, 11.36-38; 12.39-40.

15. Whether "coming into the world" modifies *man* or *light* makes no difference to our argument.

understand the eternal propositions in the mind of God. It does not come about by man's initiative or effort, but by God's, Who alone reveals truth, to whom, and when He pleases. God created man in His image, with a rational mind, to use the same laws of thought as His own. The principles of reason (logic) and knowledge are given to mankind through the *Logos*.

This being the case, whenever human beings know truth, they know that which exists in the mind of God. They do not merely have a representation of the truth, nor is truth something that stands outside both God and man to which both might have access. A Biblical epistemology denies a correspondence theory of truth, that is, that the mind of man has only a representation of the truth, and not the truth itself. Rather, a Biblical epistemology holds to a coherence theory of truth, which maintains that what man has is the truth: the same truth that exists in the mind of God. A proposition is true because God thinks it to be true. Therefore, when a man knows truth, what he knows is the same truth, the identical truth, that God knows. In this coherence theory of truth, the mind and the object known are both part of one system, a system in which all parts are in perfect accord (they "cohere"), because they are found in the mind of God.

As the *Confession* teaches, the propositional truth of special revelation is "most necessary" if one is going to come to a sound and saving knowledge of God through Jesus Christ. As Paul said: "I am not ashamed of the Gospel of Christ, for it is the power of God to salvation for everyone who believes…. Faith comes by hearing, and hearing by the Word of God" (*Romans* 1:16; 10:17). General revelation reveals God as Creator; Scripture alone reveals Him as Savior. Calvin wrote:

Scripture, gathering up the otherwise confused knowledge of God in our minds [innate ideas], having dispersed our dullness, clearly shows us the true God. This [special revelation], therefore, is a special gift, where God, to instruct the church, not merely uses mute teachers but also opens His most hallowed lips. Not only does He teach the elect to look upon a god, but also shows Himself as the God upon Whom they are to look.

God has provided the assistance of the Word for the sake of all those to whom He has been pleased to give useful instruction, because He foresaw that His likeness imprinted upon the most beautiful form of the universe would be insufficiently effective.

We must come, I say, to the Word, where God is truly and vividly described to us from His works.[16]

True knowledge, said Calvin, "is that which is delivered to us by the Law and the Prophets [Scripture]."[17] This being the case, as we will see in greater detail below, Scripture is not only necessary for salvation, it is also necessary to justify all knowledge and to interpret each and every aspect of life.

Reformed theology teaches, as expressed by the *Westminster Confession* (14:1), that "the grace of [saving] faith, whereby the elect are enabled to believe to the saving of their souls, is the work of the Spirit of Christ in their hearts, and is ordinarily wrought by the ministry of the Word." This work of God is referred to as the inner testimony of the Holy Spirit. It is an "immediate" work of the Spirit, as the *Confession* (1:5) teaches, "an inward work of the Holy Spirit bearing witness by and with the Word in our hearts." That is, Christian theology teaches, in

16. Calvin, *Institutes* I:6:1, 3.
17. Calvin, *Commentary* on *Jeremiah* 44:1-7.

contrast to the Arminian beliefs and the sacramentalism of Roman Catholicism,[18] that when the Word of God is preached, the Holy Spirit produces belief in the mind of the elect sinner without the mediation of a priest, sacrament, or human effort.

The Spirit does not (ordinarily) work in the elect sinner apart from the Word. Jesus Christ taught: "My sheep hear My voice, and I know them, and they follow Me" (*John* 10:27). Lost sinners need to hear the Gospel in order to be saved; they need to hear of Christ and His saving work. As Paul teaches in *1 Corinthians* 15:3-4, the Gospel is "good news" about actions that God the Father took, in Christ, 2000 years ago, to save elect sinners. The atonement of Jesus Christ merited salvation for the elect. The Gospel is an objective reality, grounded in the truth of the Word of God: it is, in the words of Paul, "according to the Scriptures." Yet, because it is the "Gospel of the Kingdom of God" (see *Mark* 1:14; *Matthew* 4:23), the preaching of it must include the whole counsel of God. Therefore, it is the responsibility of the church, which is "the pillar and ground of the truth" (*1 Timothy* 3:15), to preach the whole counsel of God (*Acts* 20:27), to evangelize (*2 Timothy* 4:5), and to do the work of apologetics (*1 Peter* 3:15). These are Christian duties. But the Spirit of God alone produces belief. As Paul wrote in *1 Corinthians* 3:6: "I planted, Apollos watered, but God gave the growth."

---

18. The Arminian beliefs of the Roman Catholic Church are expressed in the *Dogmatic Decrees of the Vatican Council*, Chapter III, "On Faith," where it is stated that man must cooperate with God's grace in salvation, and that faith is only the beginning of man's salvation (to be completed by good works). See Schaff, *The Creeds of Christendom*, II:242-246. And the sacramentalism of Roman Catholicism is manifest in the *Catechism of the Catholic Church* (Article 10) where it is taught that the sacraments are necessary for salvation (Doubleday, 1994).

The sinner, without any special work of God's Spirit, can sometimes understand the message preached, simply because he is the image of God. But there is a difference between understanding the truth and believing the truth. As Gordon Clark stated: "Let us agree and insist that merely to learn and understand the doctrines does not make one a Christian. Any infidel can learn and understand them quite well. In addition to understanding the doctrines one must believe them; but note that it is the doctrines that must be believed."[19] The difference, then, between faith and saving faith is that the latter is assent to, or belief in, or trust in, one or more Biblical propositions regarding Jesus Christ and His saving work.

It is also important to note that Reformed theology teaches that soteriology (the doctrine of salvation) is a branch of epistemology. It is not a branch of metaphysics, because sin is not a metaphysical problem, and men are not deified when they are saved. Neither is it a branch of ethics, for men are not saved by their own works (this is in contrast to Romanism which teaches that works are necessary to complete faith). Rather, salvation is by grace through faith alone, namely, belief in the truth as revealed by God the Spirit in His Word (*Romans* 1:16; 10:17). And this salvation is the gift of God (*Ephesians* 2:8-10).[20] This is why Reformed theology refers to Scripture as "a means of grace." As the *Shorter Catechism* (Q. 88) states, the means of grace are "the outward and ordinary means whereby Christ communicates to us the benefits of redemption, [these] are His ordinances, especially the Word, sacraments, and prayer; all of which are made effectual to the elect for salvation." Of these three "ordinances,"

19. Gordon H. Clark, *Ephesians* (The Trinity Foundation, 1985), 151.
20. John W. Robbins, "An Introduction to Gordon H. Clark," *The Trinity Review*, August 1993.

the Word is primary (*John* 8:31-32; 14:23; *1 John* 4:1-3; *2 John* 9-11) and indispensable. The Word of God is essential and necessary for salvation and sanctification. It is a means of grace in itself. The sacraments and prayer, on the other hand, are means of grace only because of the Word. That is, one cannot understand what the sacraments are apart from the Word. And for prayer to be effectual it must always be in accordance with the Word (*John* 15:7). This is why the Reformers stressed the preaching of the Word over the sacraments. By way of contrast (and a soul-damning contrast at that), Roman Catholicism stresses the sacraments as primary, believing them to be necessary for salvation.

It is also important to note that Reformed theology does not greatly separate the Law and the Gospel, though each is carefully distinguished from the other. Law without Gospel is merely a dead letter; yet there is no Gospel without the Law that reveals one's sin and his need for the grace of God in Christ. In this sense the Law has a pedagogical function: It is a "tutor" to bring us to Christ (*Galatians* 3:24). For the convert, the Law (principally the Ten Commandments) is a pattern of life; it is the unchangeable rule by which to live. It reveals the character of God and sets forth His will. It admonishes the Christian to seek and obey his God. As stated in the *Confession* (19:6): "Although true believers be not under the law as a covenant of works, to be thereby justified or condemned; yet is it of great use to them, as well as others, in that, as a rule of life, informing them of the will of God and their duty, it directs and binds them to walk accordingly." Then too, as chapter 19 of the *Westminster Confession* teaches, although the ceremonial law given to Israel "as a church under age" has been abrogated (due to the fact that it pointed to the sacrificial work of Christ, which has now been accomplished), the Ten Commandments (the moral law) along with the "general equity" of the civil or judicial law, give rules by which the three main Biblical institutions (family, church, and civil magistrate) are to be governed. These three institutions are separate and distinct entities with regard to function, but not with regard to authority. God's law is the authority for all.

Section 1 says that "it pleased the Lord, at sundry times, and in divers manners, to reveal Himself, and to declare His will unto His church [*Hebrews* 1:1-2]." This is the doctrine of progressive revelation. That is to say, Biblical revelation is progressive in nature. There is a growing body of revelation, beginning with Adam in the Garden of Eden (*Genesis* 1:26-31; 2:15-17) to the time of the apostles (*Hebrews* 2:2-4; *2 Peter* 3:1-2). In Eden, God revealed Himself to Adam in propositions, and He intermittently revealed more propositions until the close of the canon of Scripture. Throughout the entirety of the progression, the revelation is inerrant at every stage (*Psalm* 19:7). This sub-discipline of theology is referred to as Biblical theology, and it may be defined as "a study of the process of the self-revelation of God deposited in the Bible."[21] Or said another way, it is the study of the history of special revelation.

God has not chosen to reveal Himself to man all at once. Rather, revelation has an historical development. But later revelations do not always supersede earlier revelation; rather, later revelation is an addition to the revelation before it. God has seen fit to reveal Himself little by little over centuries of time: He gave some information to Adam, more to Noah, more to Abraham, more to Moses, more to David, and so forth. During these periods of time God propositionally revealed Himself and His will

---

21. Geerhardus Vos, *Biblical Theology: The Old and New Testaments* (Presbyterian and Reformed, 1948), 13.

for His church through various methods: theophanies (visible manifestations of God; *Exodus* 3); dreams (*Genesis* 37); audible voices (*Deuteronomy* 5:4); Urim and Thummim (*Numbers* 27:21; *Ezra* 2:63); and miracles and their explanations (*Exodus* 7-12; *1 Kings* 17 – *2 Kings* 8). The Word of God given to the fathers was pure (*Psalm* 19:7); it was the way of life for His people (*Deuteronomy* 10:12-13). No one was permitted to add to or delete from the Old Testament writings (*Deuteronomy* 4:2; *Proverbs* 30:5-6), a divine prohibition violated by the Roman Church-State at the Council of Trent. The sacred writings were able to lead men to a saving knowledge of Jesus Christ (*2 Timothy* 3:14-15). And according to *Hebrews* 4:2, 6, the Gospel was fully preached to Old Testament Israel.

Then too, under the Old Covenant administration, God illustrated the Gospel to Israel by means of the ceremonial law, which laws contained, says the *Confession* (19:3), "several typical ordinances, partly of worship, prefiguring Christ, His graces, actions, sufferings, and benefits." This being the case, Robert Reymond correctly stated that the Old Testament people of God "probably understood more than we are at first blush inclined to grant them."[22] And yet, as the Old Testament pointed to the coming of Christ and the New Testament age, it was incomplete (*1 Peter* 1:10-12). As the writer of *Hebrews* states: "God, Who at various times and in different ways spoke in time past to the fathers by the prophets, has in these last days spoken to us in His Son" (1:1-2). In His parable of the wicked tenant farmers (*Matthew* 21:33-44), Jesus Himself taught that He was the supreme and final revelation of God to man. But it should be made clear

22. Robert L. Reymond, *Jesus, Divine Messiah: The Old Testament Witness* (Christian Focus Publications, 1990), 100-101.

that the "Son revelation" necessarily includes and must never be separated from Christ's revelation through His apostles, that is, the New Testament documents. As Jesus stated, His Holy Spirit would be the One speaking in and through the apostles whom Christ chose (*Matthew* 10:40; *John* 15:26-27). It is the Word of God incarnate Who, through the writings of the apostles, gave us the finalized Word of God wholly inscripturated (more will be said on this below).

The Bible itself bears witness to the intermittent growth of revelation. We read in *Exodus* 31:18 that God "gave Moses two tablets of the Testimony, tablets of stone, written by the finger of God [the Holy Spirit]."[23] These tablets were placed in the ark of the covenant (*Deuteronomy* 10:5; *Hebrews* 9:4). But then in *Deuteronomy* 31:24-26 we are told that "when Moses had completed writing the words of this law in a book [the book of *Deuteronomy*]...[it was to be] put beside the ark of the covenant." In other words, under the inspiration of the Spirit, Moses wrote additional words, adding to the canon. Other references to Moses writing the words of the Pentateuch are found in *Exodus* 24:4; 34:27; *Numbers* 33:2; and *Deuteronomy* 31:22. After the death of Moses the canon was expanded when Joshua "wrote these words in the book of the Law of God" (*Joshua* 24:26). Later in the history of Israel, some of Samuel's writings were added to the canon when "he wrote [certain words] in a book and laid it up before the Lord" (*1 Samuel* 10:25). In *1 Chronicles* 29:29 we are told that Samuel, Nathan, and Gad wrote about "the acts of king David." In *2 Chronicles* 26:22 we read that Isaiah the prophet wrote down "the rest of the acts of Uzziah."

---

23. When we compare *Matthew* 12:28 with *Luke* 11:20, we see that the phrase "the finger of God" is a periphrasis for the Holy Spirit.

And in *2 Chronicles* 32:32, the same prophet inscripturated for us "the rest of the acts of Hezekiah." Then in *Jeremiah* 30:2 God told the prophet Jeremiah to "write in a book for yourself all the words that I have spoken to you." And in *Revelation* 1:11 we read that John is told to "write in a book" the things which are about to be revealed to him. These are just samples of those numerous passages that attest to the fact that there is an episodic growth of written revelation witnessed to by the Bible itself.[24] The Bible recounts its own growth to maturity.

Another way that progressive revelation is recognizable in the Bible is in the various covenants that God has instituted and established with His people. The Scriptures teach only two covenants in which God has chosen to interact with mankind: the covenant of works and the covenant of grace. In accordance with Reformed theology, the *Westminster Confession* (7:2) teaches that when God created man He entered into a covenant of works with him: "The first covenant made with man was a covenant of works, wherein life was promised to Adam, and in him [as the federal head of the entire human race] to his posterity, upon perfect and personal obedience." As we read in *Romans* 5, however, Adam disobeyed God. And as he was the federal, covenantal, representative, and biological head of all mankind, his first sin was imputed to all his ordinary descendants. As stated in the *Westminster Shorter Catechism* (Q. 16): "The covenant being made with Adam, not only for himself, but for his posterity; all mankind, descending from him by ordinary generation, sinned in him, and fell with him, in his first transgression."

24. See also *2 Chronicles* 9:29; 12:15; *Isaiah* 30:8; *Jeremiah* 29:1; 36:1-32; 45:1; *Ezekiel* 43:11; *Daniel* 7:1; and *Habakkuk* 2:2; for more on this, see Wayne Grudem, *Systematic Theology: An Introduction to Biblical Doctrine* (Zondervan, 1994), 54-55.

All men, therefore, as a result of Adam's first sin, are judicially guilty.[25] Adam's sin was imputed to all, because Adam was the legal representative of all. But as the *Shorter Catechism* (Q. 20) teaches, God did not leave all mankind to perish in this state: "God having, out of His mere good pleasure, from all eternity, elected some to everlasting life, did enter into a covenant of grace, to deliver them out of the estate of sin and misery, and to bring them into an estate of salvation by a Redeemer." This Redeemer is Jesus Christ. And the covenant of grace, as the *Larger Catechism* (Q. 31) says, "was made with Christ as the second Adam, and in Him with all the elect as His seed." Reformed theology maintains that there is one covenant of grace that runs throughout the entirety of the Bible. As stated in the *Confession* (7:5-6): This one covenant "was differently administered in the time of the Law [Old Testament], and the time of the Gospel [New Testament]." Nevertheless, there are not "two covenants of grace differing in substance, but one and the same under the various dispensations."

The covenant of grace was initially revealed in *Genesis* 3:15 with the first Messianic or "Gospel promise" (the *protoevangelium*), directly subsequent to the fall. According to the *Confession* (7:3):

> Man by his fall having made himself incapable of life by that covenant [of works], the Lord was pleased to make a second, commonly called the covenant of grace; whereby He freely offers unto sinners life and salvation by Jesus Christ, requiring of them faith in Him, that they may be saved.

25. Jesus Christ, of course, is excluded from this judicial guilt, because as the second and last Adam (*1 Corinthians* 15:45-47), He did not descend from Adam "by ordinary generation."

As Paul teaches in *Ephesians* 2:12, there is a thematic unity of all the covenants; he writes of "the covenants" (plural) of "the promise" (singular). "The promise" is salvation. With the coming of the New Covenant, "the promise" that ran through the entirety of the Old Covenant reached its fulfillment with the advent of the Redeemer Himself: Jesus Christ. As the New Testament teaches, Christ accomplished redemption on behalf of His people, thus bringing to fruition all of the types of the earlier dispensation of the covenant of grace (*Hebrews* 8-10). Christ is the "Amen" to all of the promises of God (*2 Corinthians* 1:20). In Him all things "which are written in the *Law of Moses* and the *Prophets* and the *Psalms*" reach their fulfillment (*Luke* 24:44). Thus, as Gordon Clark stated, the Old and New Testament Scriptures are to be viewed "as a developing body of revelation – developing from a less detailed to a more detailed form – of a single plan of salvation."[26] Special revelation, then, in both the Old and New Testaments, is both redemptive and progressive. The New Covenant is superior or greater, not so much in content, as in administration ("in Christ," rather than via the ceremonial law) and detail.

Then, too, as Section 1 teaches, God not only chose "to reveal Himself, and to declare His will unto His church," but "afterward, for the better preserving and propagating of the truth, and for the more sure establishment and comfort of the church against the corruption of the flesh, the malice of Satan and of the world, to commit the same wholly unto writing: which makes the Holy Scripture to be most necessary; those former ways of God's revealing His will unto His people being now ceased."

26. Gordon H. Clark, *The Atonement* (The Trinity Foundation [1987] 1996), 17.

Warfield pointed out that it is due to the insufficiency of general or natural revelation that God in His goodness gave His church special revelation. But the goodness of God was not "exhausted in merely making known the saving truth unto men; He took means to preserve the knowledge of it and to propagate it."[27] That is to say, written revelation would be less likely to be lost, distorted, perverted, forgotten, augmented, or supplemented than mere oral tradition. The Apostle Peter teaches this in his second epistle, when he states that the written Word of God is "more sure" than the voice of God from Heaven (*2 Peter* 1:16-19). It is not that the audible voice of God is a lesser revelation than the written Word, but it is temporary, and not durable. The audible voice is temporary; the written Word is permanent. Herein is the superiority of the Word of God written; it gives us stability and certainty. This is why Luke writes that he has written his *Gospel* in order "that you may know the *certainty* of those words in which you were instructed" (*Luke* 1:1-4). Solomon makes the same claim: "Have I not *written* to you excellent things...that I may make you know the *certainty* of the words of truth?" (*Proverbs* 22:20-21).

According to the Westminster divines, in direct contrast with Roman Catholicism, and other nominally Christian groups that add to or take away from the Word of God, the written Word of God ("Holy Scripture") is "most necessary." It is necessary, not only "unto salvation," it is also necessary to propagate the truth, to establish and comfort the church against her enemies in this world, and to ensure that God's will be properly declared unto His church. Or said another way, the Word of God written is necessary for the justification of all knowledge. The reason for

27. Warfield, *The Westminster Assembly and Its Work*, 194.

this necessity is that the canon of Scripture is now closed: "those former ways of God's revealing His will unto His people being now ceased."

Since special revelation has ceased, and general revelation is inadequate, one must go to the written Word if he would seek to know the way of God unto salvation and the will of God for His church. To deny this principle by adding to (as Roman Catholicism with its "traditions", and the Charismatic movement with its "prophecy"), or deleting from (as with ultra-dispensationalism on one hand and liberalism on the other), the Word of God, is to abandon the Scriptural principle of *sola Scriptura*. It is to vitiate the teaching of the Word of God itself. As taught by the *Confession* (1:6): "The whole counsel of God concerning all things necessary for His own glory, man's salvation, faith, and life, is either expressly set down in Scripture, or by good and necessary consequence may be deduced from Scripture: unto which nothing at any time is to be added, whether by new revelations of the Spirit or traditions of men."

The Identity of Scripture

1:2 Under the name of Holy Scripture, or the Word of God written, are now contained all the books of the Old and New Testaments, which are these:

Of the Old Testament:

Genesis	Ruth	Ezra
Exodus	1 Samuel	Nehemiah
Leviticus	2 Samuel	Esther
Numbers	1 Kings	Job
Deuteronomy	2 Kings	Psalms
Joshua	1 Chronicles	Proverbs
Judges	2 Chronicles	Ecclesiastes

Song of Songs	Hosea	Nahum
Isaiah	Joel	Habakkuk
Jeremiah	Amos	Zephaniah
Lamentations	Obadiah	Haggai
Ezekiel	Jonah	Zechariah
Daniel	Micah	Malachi

Of the New Testament:

Matthew	Ephesians	Hebrews
Mark	Philippians	James
Luke	Colossians	1 Peter
John	1 Thessalonians	2 Peter
Acts	2 Thessalonians	1 John
Romans	1 Timothy	2 John
1 Corinthians	2 Timothy	3 John
2 Corinthians	Titus	Jude
Galatians	Philemon	Revelation

All of which are given by inspiration of God to be the rule of faith and life.

1:3 The books commonly called the *Apocrypha*,[28] not being of divine inspiration, are no part of the canon of Scripture, and therefore are of no authority in the church of God, nor to be any otherwise approved, or made use of, than other human writings.

The final statement of Section 1 has to do with the close of the canon of Scripture, and leads us into Sections 2 and 3, where the canon is denotatively defined as the 66 books of the Old and New Testaments.

28. The word *Apocrypha* derives from the Greek *apokrupha*, which means "hidden things."

The word "canon" derives from the Greek *kanon*, which means "rule" or "measuring rod" (as in *Galatians* 6:16; *2 Corinthians* 10:13; and *Philippians* 3:16). When Protestants speak of the "canon" they are speaking about the rule of faith and practice which is found in the 66 books of the Bible. As stated by William Whitaker: "The books of Scripture are called canonical because they contain the standard and rule of our faith and morals…they prescribe to us what we must believe, and how we ought to live…. Hence too, we may perceive that the Scripture is perfect, since otherwise the title of canon or rule could hardly be applied to it."[29]

Thus, whereas Roman Catholicism holds that the rule of faith and practice for the church is found in the Bible (including the *Apocrypha*[30]) as interpreted by church tradition,[31] Protestantism insists that the (66 book) Bible and the Bible alone is the Word of God. The Biblical doctrine of progressive revelation maintains that the canon of Scripture was closed at the end of the apostolic age (probably prior to A.D. 70, but certainly no later than A.D. 100). The Old Testament writings were finalized around 400 B.C. (with *Malachi*). Some 400 years later God began to speak to His people again through the angel Gabriel (*Luke* 1), dreams (*Matthew* 1-2), and John the Baptist (*Matthew* 3). Then

29. William Whitaker, *A Disputation on Holy Scripture*, 27-28.

30. The Roman Church-State's Bible consists of the 66 books of the Old and New Testaments plus the following books of the *Apocrypha*: *Tobit, Judith, 1 and 2 Maccabees, the Wisdom of Solomon, Sirach* [or *Ecclesiasticus*], and *Baruch;* see *Catechism of the Catholic Church*, paragraph 120. The Roman Church sometimes refers to these as *deuterocanonical* rather than *Apocryphal.* What Romanism intends by this is to assert that these books were "later added to the canon" by the Church.

31. See the *Dogmatic Decrees of the Vatican Council*, Chapter II, "Of Revelation"; Schaff, *The Creeds of Christendom*, II:240-242.

when "the fullness of the times" came (*Ephesians* 1:10), God spoke through the sending of His Son, the Word of God incarnate (*John* 1:14, 18; *Hebrews* 1:1-2).

Christ personally validated the canon of Palestinian Judaism, which consisted of 22 books of the Hebrew Old Testament, which correspond to the 39 books of the Protestant Old Testament. He did not, on the other hand, validate the *Apocrypha.* In *Luke* 24:44, for example, Christ clearly alludes to the tripartite division of the Hebrew Old Testament: "the *Law of Moses,* and the *Prophets,* and the *Psalms* [that is, the Writings]," intentionally avoiding any reference to, and excluding the *Apocrypha* from the Old Testament.

Christ then commissioned His apostles (*Matthew* 10:1-4), and as Robert Reymond states, "pre-authenticated their spoken [*2 Peter* 3:1-2] and written [*1 Corinthians* 14:37; *1 Thessalonians* 2:13] Word."[32] In *John* 14:26 and 16:12-15, Christ promised that the Holy Spirit (the *Parakletos,* Helper or Comforter) would oversee both the production of the *Gospels* and the balance of the New Testament writings.

Christ also endowed His apostles with certain miraculous gifts which confirmed their message as of divine origin (*Matthew* 10:7-8; *Mark* 16:20; *2 Corinthians* 12:12). Only these men (and those with apostolic authority, sanction, or endorsement, such as Luke and Mark) were commissioned for this task. They alone were Christ's representatives (*Matthew* 10:40). The authoritative words of these apostolic men composed the "deposit" (*2 Timothy* 1:12) or "tradition" (*1 Corinthians* 11:2; *2 Thessalonians* 2:15) to which the church was to adhere (and not the "traditions" of the later Roman Church-State).

32. Reymond, *A New Systematic Theology of the Christian Faith,* 61.

Thus, when the final apostle died, or laid down his "apostolic pen," the giving of special revelation ceased. *Second Timothy* 3:16-17 further attest to this fact when they claim that the completed Scripture (the 66 books of the Bible) thoroughly equips us "for every good work." By implication, then, there is and can be no extra-Biblical special divine revelation. The canon of Scripture is closed: "those former ways [miracles, tongues, spoken prophecy, visions, theophanies, dreams, angelic visits] of God's revealing His will unto His people being now ceased."

Leonard Coppes addressed the issue of the closing of the canon as follows:

> The primary verses teaching this are *John* 14:26, *Ephesians* 2:20, *Jude* 3 and 20. The first verse teaches that Jesus committed the truth to the apostolate alone. So when the apostolate ceased, so did the flow of divine revelation. The second verse teaches that the communicators of divine revelation…were the apostles and the prophets alone. With the cessation of the apostolate (and the Scriptures acknowledge that the apostolate did cease) the communication of new revelation ceased. The last two verses (as well as *Ephesians* 2:20) teach that the church is to be built on the faith (the revelation communicated to the apostolate and through the apostles and prophets) which was once for all delivered to the saints and on nothing else. We are neither to add to this faith nor subtract from it. All questions of faith and life are to be submitted to the authority of the Scripture. Men are not free to create new revelation nor are they free to reject any teaching or command recorded in Scripture. To do so is to oppose the authority of God.[33]

33. Leonard J. Coppes, *Are Five Points Enough? Ten Points of Calvinism* (Leonard J. Coppes, 1980), 2-3.

The close of the canon of Scripture, that is, the cessation of divine propositional revelation, is also explicitly taught in *1 Corinthians* 13:8-13.[34] In this passage Paul is dealing with the miraculous word gifts in the visible church, just as in chapters 12 and 14. What is their purpose and duration? The apostle says they have a place, but they are a partial means of revelation (verses 9-10). When the "perfect" or "complete" or "mature" (*teleios*) comes, then the partial will be done away with (verse 10). Paul is contrasting that which is complete and endures with that which is partial and temporary. The fully written Word of God is complete (and perfect) and endures forever (*1 Peter* 1:24-25). The Scripture is frequently referred to as perfect and complete (*James* 1:25; *2 Timothy* 3:16-17). It is an all-sufficient Word.

Prior to the completion of the writing, lesser means of revelation were still useful. Before the writing was complete, God's people saw "as in a mirror dimly." But by the time that all of Scripture was completed, they would know fully all that God has chosen to reveal (verse 12). The miraculous word-gifts were for the apostolic age of the church (verse 11; 14:20-21). Paul is preparing the church for the coming of the completed revelation of God: a time when they would leave behind the partial.

Daniel 9 gives us a Biblical *terminus ad quem* ("a finishing point") for the Old Testament sacrificial system and the partial means of revelation.[35] Daniel prophesies that when the Messiah

34. See Gordon H. Clark, *First Corinthians* (The Trinity Foundation [1975] 1991), 211-217; Robert L. Reymond, *What About Continuing Revelations and Miracles in the Presbyterian Church Today?* (Presbyterian and Reformed, 1977), 30-36; and Jonathan Edwards, *Charity and Its Fruits* (The Banner of Truth Trust [1969] 1986), 304-322.

35. See John Gill, *Exposition of the Old and New Testaments* (The Baptist Standard Bearer, 1989), VI:344; and Wayne Jackson, "Daniel's Prophecy of the Seventy Weeks," *Reason and Revelation* (Apologetics Press, July 1997).

is cut off in the seventieth week (verse 26), the sacrificial system would no longer be necessary (verse 27). Sin would once for all time be atoned for and everlasting righteousness merited (verse 24). This, of course, occurred in the vicarious atonement of Jesus Christ (*Matthew* 27:51; *John* 19:30; *Hebrews* 9:28). But Daniel also states that prior to the coming abomination of desolation (verse 27), all visions and prophecies (the miraculous word-gifts) would cease (verse 24). The canon of Scripture would be closed. Jesus defines the abomination of desolation as the Roman armies under Titus, as they surrounded Jerusalem in A.D. 70 (compare *Matthew* 24:15 with *Luke* 21:20-24). Daniel and Paul are in agreement: The canon of Scripture would be closed by the end of the apostolic age. And they both teach that the partial means of revelation would cease at that time. The church now has the completed canon in the 66 books of the Bible.

Calvin said it this way:

> God will not speak intermittently through some and through others; nor will He add prophecies to prophecies, or revelations to revelations. Rather, He has so fulfilled all functions of teaching in His Son that we must regard this as the final and eternal testimony from Him. In this way, the whole New Testament time, from the point that Christ appeared to us with the preaching of His Gospel even to the Day of Judgment, is designated by "the last hour"… "the last times"… "the last days." This is done that, content with the perfection of Christ's teaching, we may learn not to fashion anything new for ourselves beyond this or to admit anything contrived by others.[36]

The position taught by the Westminster Assembly that divine revelation is confined to the 66 books of the Old and New

36. Calvin, *Institutes* IV:8:7.

Testaments is by no means unique among Protestant creedal statements.[37]

The *French Confession* of 1559 (III, V) teaches that:

> These Holy Scriptures are comprised in the [66] canonical books of the Old and New Testaments.
>
> And inasmuch as [the Bible] is the rule of all truth ... it is not lawful for men, nor even angels, to add to it, to take away from it, or to change it.

The *Belgic Confession* of 1561 (II, VII) states that:

> [God] makes Himself ... known to us by His Holy and divine Word; that is to say, as far as it is necessary for us to know in this life, to His glory and our salvation.
>
> We believe that these [66 books of the] Holy Scriptures fully contain the will of God, and that whatsoever man ought to believe unto salvation is sufficiently taught therein...it is unlawful for anyone, though an apostle, to teach otherwise than we are now taught in the Holy Scriptures...since it is forbidden to add unto or take away anything from the Word of God.

The *Second Helvetic Confession* of 1566 (I) declares:

> We believe and confess the [66 books of the] canonical Scriptures of the holy prophets and apostles of both Testaments to be the true Word of God.
>
> And in this Holy Scripture, the universal church has all things fully expounded which belong to a saving faith, and also to the framing of a life acceptable to God; and in this respect it is expressly commanded of God that nothing be either put to or taken from the same.

37. See Schaff, *The Creeds of Christendom*, III: Part Second.

The *Formula of Concord* of 1577 (I) claims:

> We believe, confess, and teach that the only rule and norm, according to which all dogmas and all doctors ought to be esteemed and judged, is no other whatever than the prophetic and apostolic writings both of the Old and New Testaments.
>
> But other writings, whether of the fathers or of the moderns, with whatever name they come, are in no wise to be [considered] equal to the Holy Scriptures, but are all to be esteemed inferior to them, so that they be not otherwise received than in the rank of witnesses, to show what doctrine was taught after the apostles' times also, and in what parts of the world that more sound doctrine of the prophets and apostles has been preserved.

The *Irish Articles of Religion* of 1615 (1, 6) read:

> The ground of our religion and the rule of faith and all saving truth is the Word of God, contained in the [66 books of] Holy Scripture.
>
> The Holy Scriptures contain all things necessary to salvation, and are able to instruct sufficiently in all points of faith that we are bound to believe, and all good duties that we are bound to practice.

The *Savoy Declaration* of 1658 and the *1689 Baptist Confession of Faith* make virtually the same pronouncements regarding Scripture that we find in the *Westminster Confession of Faith*. From these statements it is clear that Protestant confessionalism adheres to the Scriptural principle of *sola Scriptura*, while Roman Catholicism renounces it.

Numerous Scripture passages can be adduced to support the view taught by the Westminster Assembly. In *Psalm* 1:2-3 we are told that the blessed man is one who "delights in the Law [written revelation] of the Lord, and in His Law he meditates day and night," thus teaching the sufficiency of Scripture. In *Psalm* 19:7 we read that "the Law [Scripture] of the Lord is perfect," that is, adequate, sufficient, and without error. And the whole of *Psalm* 119 is dedicated to the teaching that it is God's Law which is without defect, which alone is to be loved, meditated upon, and practiced.

As we have seen, in *2 Timothy* 3:16-17 Paul declares that "all Scripture" (the 66 books of the Bible) *thoroughly* equips the man of God "for *every* good work" (emphasis added). In *2 Peter* 1:3-4 we are taught that the study of theology (as found in the teachings of the "holy prophets and the commandment of us the apostles," that is, the Old and New Testaments; *2 Peter* 3:2) gives "to us *all things* that pertain to life and godliness" (emphasis added). In *Acts* 20:26-27, 32, Paul teaches that "the whole counsel of God" is found in God's Word, "which [alone] is able to build you up and give you an inheritance among those who are sanctified." In *Romans* 2:20 Paul states that "the form of knowledge and truth" is found in "the Law." In *Romans* 4:3, to settle the matter of justification by grace through faith alone the apostle appeals to the Word of God alone: "For what does the Scripture say?" In *1 Corinthians* 4:6, Paul enjoins his readers "not to think beyond what is written." And in *Acts* 17:11 the same apostle commends the Bereans because they were ready to test all things, including the words of an apostle, by Scripture alone. In *John* 17:17, when Christ defines truth for His apostles, He asserts that "[God's] Word is truth." Note that Christ does not merely say that God's Word is true (*alethes*). Rather, He uses the noun *aletheia* (truth). In other words, the Lord is saying that God's Word is the truth itself. Then, too, when Jesus tells His auditors where they must go to find eternal life He states: "Search the

Scriptures...these are they which testify of Me" (*John* 5:39).[38] In *John* 10:35 Christ says that it is "the Scriptures [which] cannot be broken." In *Matthew* 22:29 He rebukes the Sadducees who err "not knowing the Scriptures." And very significant is the *Acts* 15 passage concerning the Jerusalem council. When the apostles and elders met to discuss and make a judgment regarding the theological matter of circumcision and its necessity with regard to salvation, they did not quote inspired tradition, neither did they turn to a bishop or pope for a decision on the matter. And even though the council was made up in part of apostles, the delegates believed themselves compelled to cite Scripture (*Amos* 9:11-12) to settle the matter (*Acts* 15:15-16). The conclusion reached by the council was based on the fact that "it seemed good to the Holy Spirit [the author of *Amos* 9:11-12] and to us" (verse 32). Scripture and Scripture alone rendered the decision binding on the local churches (*Acts* 16:4).

Surely Boettner was correct when he claimed that the doctrine of *sola Scriptura* as taught by the Protestants "is everywhere assumed" in the Bible.[39] As stated in the *Larger Catechism* (Q. 3): "The Holy Scriptures of the Old and New Testaments are the Word of God, the *only* rule of faith and obedience" [emphasis added]. Reformed theology, Roman Catholicism, and Pentecostalism could hardly be more at odds on this issue.

As we have seen, the Roman Church-State teaches that the Bible is the infallible and inerrant Word of God. But just as the Romanist word *Bible* does not mean what Christians mean by the same word, so in its mouth the words *infallible* and *inerrant*

38. Whether the verb "search" is in the indicative or imperative mood, the meaning is the same regarding the fact that the knowledge of Christ is to be found only in the Scriptures.

39. Loraine Boettner, *Roman Catholicism*, 92.

do not mean what Christians mean. Rome includes the *Apocrypha* in the Bible and declares that alongside the written Word there is also the unwritten Word, the oral tradition that is found in the (written!) pronouncements of the church councils and papal decrees issued by the Magisterium, the teaching authority of the church. These are of equal authority. Or better, they are simply different forms of the same inchoate Word. However, in the view of Romanism, the Roman Church-State, with the pope being considered the spiritual successor of the Apostle Peter and the Vicar of Christ on Earth, is the only infallible interpreter of Scripture,[40] and tradition takes precedence over the Bible. The Bible is what the Roman Church-State says it is.

As expressed in the *Westminster Confession of Faith*, on the other hand, Christian theology rejects both the *Apocrypha* and tradition (oral or written) as having authority equal with Scripture. This is not to say that the *Apocrypha* and tradition have no value; it is simply that they do not have any more authority than any other human writings. Says the *Confession:* The *Apocrypha* is "of no authority in the church of God, nor to be any otherwise approved, or made use of, than other human writings."

The same is true with the traditions that have been handed down from the early church theologians. There may be some value in studying them. This is why the Protestant church through the years has developed creeds and confessions, such as the one we are presently studying. A creed or confession is a summary and orderly statement about what the church believes concerning Christian doctrine. As standards subordinate to the Word of

40. See *The Canons and Decrees of the Council of Trent,* Fourth Session; and *Dogmatic Decrees of the Vatican Council,* Third Session, chapters I-II, Fourth Session, chapters I-IV; Schaff, *The Creeds of Christendom,* II:79-82; II:234-271.

God, creeds serve as distillations of the teaching of Scripture, and are useful in Christian education. Too, they serve as guards against heresy. In Reformed churches, the *Westminster Confession of Faith* functions as a paradigm that provides boundaries, acting as a filter to screen theological teachings. All teaching is run through the "grid" or the paradigm of the *Confession*.

In these ways creeds and confessions are very useful. This is the sense in which Augustine once wrote: "The sentiments of the bishops who have gone before us, men who treated these divine words [of Scripture] faithfully and memorably...what they found in the church, they held; what they had learned, they taught; what they had received from the fathers, this they delivered to the children."[41] But never are creeds and confessions to be considered on a par with Scripture. Rather, they, like the decisions of synods and councils, says the *Confession* (31:4), may and do err: "therefore they are not to be made the rule of faith or practice; but to be used as a help in both." The Bible and the Bible alone is the Word of God, the only infallible, inerrant standard by which all is to be judged.

There are a number of reasons that the Protestant churches reject the apocryphal books as the Word of God.[42] First, they were never part of the Palestinian Canon, which Jesus and the apostles adopted. We have no record of Christ and the apostles quoting from them. Significantly, in the New Testament there are over 500 references to the Old Testament writings (either

41. Augustine, *Against Julian*, 2, 19:34; as cited by Joseph Gallegos in *Not By Scripture Alone*, 390.

42. See Boettner, *Roman Catholicism*, 80-87; William Hendriksen, *Survey of the Bible* (Baker Book House [1947] 1976), 20-22; and Norman L. Geisler and William E. Nix, *A General Introduction to the Bible* (Moody Press [1968] 1986), 264-275.

direct quotes or allusions), yet there is not a single reference to any book of the *Apocrypha*. In fact, as we have seen, in *Luke* 24:44 Jesus' mention of "the *Law of Moses* and the *Prophets* and the *Psalms*" is almost certainly alluding to the tripartite division of the Hebrew Old Testament, and therefore constitutes a rejection of the *Apocrypha* as a part of Scripture.

Second, the Jewish historian Flavius Josephus did not include the apocryphal books in his list of the Hebrew Scriptures.[43] Even though he knew of these writings, he said they were "not … worthy of equal credit" with the Old Testament books.[44]

Third, the early church theologians, with the (questionable) exception of Augustine, declared emphatically that the *Apocrypha* was not to be considered a part of the Word of God. And even Augustine, although he did give some credence to the *Apocrypha* as a part of the canon, due to his high regard for the *Septuagint*, he did so in a secondary sense. That is, the apocryphal books were always approached with less reverence than the Old Testament books themselves. Or said another way, for Augustine the *Apocrypha* was, at best, deuterocanonical. In Augustine's own words: "However, the writings not included in the Jewish canon [which was the 39 Old Testament books which Protestants affirm today] do not carry as much weight as the canonical books when put forward as evidence against the opposition."[45] Later, in his *Retractions*, Augustine moved even further away from his earlier high opinion of the *Apocrypha*, and rejected some of his prior

43. Josephus, *Against Apion*, 1:37-43.
44. Josephus, *Against Apion*, 1:41.
45. Augustine, *City of God* 17.20; see also Whitaker, *A Disputation on Holy Scripture*, 45-49; and Norman L. Geisler, editor, *What Augustine Says* (Baker Book House, 1982), 44-48.

thoughts.[46] W. G. T. Shedd wrote: "Augustine adopts the Protestant, and opposes the Papal theory of tradition and authority."[47]

Fourth, even Jerome, the translator of the Latin *Vulgate* (the official Roman Catholic Bible), which contains the *Apocrypha*, denied that the *Apocrypha* was in any sense to be thought of as a part of the Old Testament.

Fifth, some of the apocryphal works themselves disclaim inspiration (see the prologue to *Ecclesiasticus*; *1 Maccabees* 4:46; 9:27; *2 Maccabees* 2:23; 15:38).

Sixth, historical errors and falsehoods are found in some of the books.

Seventh, it can hardly be doubted that when the Council of Trent (in 1546) pronounced (some of) the apocryphal books canonical, it did so after the fact, in order to support some of the heretical doctrines of Roman Catholicism (such as purgatory, salvation by works, prayers for the dead, etc.) not found in the 66 books of the Bible.

E. J. Young wrote:

> There are no marks in these [apocryphal] books which would attest a divine origin.
>
> Both *Judith* and *Tobit* contain historical, chronological, and geographical errors. The books justify falsehood and deception and make salvation to depend upon works of merit.
>
> *Ecclesiasticus* and the *Wisdom of Solomon* inculcate a morality based upon expediency. *Wisdom* teaches the creation of the world out of pre-existent matter (11:17). *Ecclesiasticus* teaches that the giving of alms makes atonement for sin (3:30). In *Baruch* it is said that God hears the prayers of the

46. Augustine, *Retractions* 1.30; 2.4; see also Geisler, *What Augustine Says*, 44-48.
47. Cited in Warfield, *Calvin and Augustine*, 465.

dead (3:4), and in *1 Maccabees* there are historical and geo-graphical errors.[48]

As noted, not only does Romanism violate the direct teaching of Scripture itself (*Deuteronomy* 4:2; *Proverbs* 30:6; *Revelation* 22:18-19), by adding to the Word of God with the inclusion of the *Apocrypha*, it also adds to Scripture with its traditions. These alleged infallible traditions come from the Roman Church-State, as the only genuine interpreter of the Bible. Regarding the matter of church tradition, Roman Catholicism insists that "the New Testament itself demonstrates the process of living tradition."[49] That is, Rome is asseverating that all it is doing is following the teaching of the Bible. Of course, it is true that the New Testament speaks favorably of some tradition (*1 Corinthians* 11:2; *2 Thessalonians* 2:15; 3:6), as well as unfavorably of other tradition; but the only tradition mentioned favorably is the teaching of the apostles themselves. As Robert Reymond points out, "it is a giant leap in logic simply to assert, because there was such a thing as 'apostolic tradition' in the New Testament age, that that tradition justifies the positing of an ongoing 'process of living tradition' after the close of the New Testament canon."[50] Until Scripture was completed, special revelation was inchoate. After it was completed, oral tradition disappeared (there never was any "living tradition"), and the only authority is the infallible and inerrant written Word of God, which contains all the apostolic tradition.

The Bible itself condemns non-apostolic religious tradition. In *Mark* 7 and *Matthew* 15, Christ strongly rebuke the Pharisees

48. Edward J. Young, "The Canon of the Old Testament," in *Revelation and the Bible*, edited by Carl F. H. Henry (Tyndale Press, 1959), 167-168.
49. The *Catechism of the Catholic Church*, paragraph 83.
50. Reymond, *A New Systematic Theology of the Christian Faith*, 85.

for rejecting the commandments of God by holding fast the traditions of men. The traditions were religious traditions regarded as authoritative by the leaders of the Jewish church. Paul too warned against being led astray by the traditions of men in *Colossians* 2:8. And in *1 Corinthians* 4:6 he enjoined the church "not to think beyond what is written," thereby issuing a warning against accepting traditions, religious, ecclesiastical, or otherwise, as authoritative or as the Word of God.

It needs to be stated again here that the Westminster Assembly is not inveighing against the usefulness of some traditions. What the Assembly is opposing, and correctly so, is tradition being accorded any authority as a rule of faith and practice. The only traditions the Bible does tell us to heed are the teachings of the apostles, which are now found in the Bible alone (*1 Corinthians* 11:2; *2 Thessalonians* 2:15). They alone have authority.

Rome, of course, claims that her traditions are apostolic, and therefore infallible, in that the line of popes is "descended" from Peter. Scripture, however, points out that an apostle of Christ was one who had seen the resurrected Christ (*Acts* 1:21-22; *1 Corinthians* 9:1), and had been directly called by Him (*Matthew* 10:1-4; *Acts* 9:1-16), a claim no man in the past 19 centuries can truthfully make. Further, in *1 Corinthians* 15:8, Paul teaches that he was the final apostle. The Romanists' claim to the apostolate, therefore, is anti-Biblical. The tradition of "apostolic succession" is an ecclesiastical fiction that contradicts the Word of God.

Moreover, Romanism's assertion that the pope is the Vicar of Christ on Earth is so audacious an error that it should be immediately recognized as such by anyone who has even the slightest knowledge of the Bible. The Apostle John's third letter, for instance, strongly warns against the establishment of monepiscopal rule (*3 John* 9-10). Too, when Cornelius fell down before Peter

(Rome's alleged first pope) as an act of obeisance, Peter flatly denied that he was in any sense the Vicar of Christ, and (mildly) rebuked Cornelius for his actions (*Acts* 10:24-26). Nevertheless, in effect, what is being asserted here is that the pope is God on Earth. In 1075, Pope Gregory VII claimed "That the Roman Church was founded by God alone.... That the Roman Pontiff alone is rightly to be called universal.... That his [the pope's] title is unique in the world.... That he [the pope] himself may be judged by no one." Thomas Aquinas wrote about the pope that he "is the successor of St. Peter, Vicar of Christ, the Roman Pontiff, to whom all kings must be subject just as they are subject to our Lord Jesus." And Vicar General Preston stated that: "Every word that [Pope] Leo [XIII] speaks from his high chair is the voice of the Holy Ghost and must be obeyed."[51]

Statements like these make it readily understandable why the Protestant Reformers considered the papacy to be the Antichrist, in accordance with *2 Thessalonians* 2:1-12. Christ is the only mediator between God and men (*1 Timothy* 2:5). He is the only high priest (*Hebrews* 7-10) and shepherd of His people (*1 Peter* 2:24-25). As the *Westminster Confession* (25:6) clearly states: "There is no other head of the church but the Lord Jesus Christ; nor can the pope of Rome, in any sense, be head thereof; but is that Antichrist, that man of sin, and son of perdition, that exalts himself in the church, against Christ and all that is called God."

Romanism maintains that the divine work of "authenticating miracles" still occurs today through the Roman Church-State (for example, the miracle of the Mass, or the miracles

---

51. These quotes are cited in John W. Robbins, *Ecclesiastical Megalomania: The Economic and Political Thought of the Roman Catholic Church* (The Trinity Foundation, 1999), 119, 129, 149n.

performed by "saints").[52] The Protestant view, on the other hand, is that the completion of Scripture means that the age of divine miracles has ceased (*1 Corinthians* 13:8-13). Prior to the close of the canon in the first century, God used miracles as a means of authenticating his messengers and the message they proclaimed. This was seen during the Mosaic era in *Exodus* 7-10. During the times of the prophets we read about such authenticating miracles in *1 Kings* 17:17-24 and 18:36-39. In the New Testament we read of Jesus' miracles of turning the water into wine (*John* 2:1-12), calming the storm (*Mark* 4:35-41), healing the incurable (*Mark* 2:1-12), and raising the dead (*John* 11:1-44). Christ then commissioned His apostles and authenticated their ministry by granting them certain miraculous gifts (*Matthew* 10:8; *Acts* 14:3; *2 Corinthians* 12:12; *Hebrews* 2:2-4). As these ambassadors of Christ went forth to fulfill the Great Commission, their preaching was confirmed by "accompanying signs" (*Mark* 16:20). Thus, as Reymond says: "The miracles of the Old Testament age authenticated Moses and the prophets as men of God.... And the miracles of the New Testament age authenticated in turn Christ and His apostles as the bearers of this new corpus of revelation."[53]

---

52. The alleged miracle of the Mass is called "transubstantiation." The theory is that even though the sensible qualities of the bread and wine remain the same, by the miraculous pronouncement of the administering priest, the elements become in substance the actual body and blood of Christ. See "The Canons and Decrees of the Council of Trent," Thirteenth Session; Schaff, *The Creeds of Christendom*, II:126-139. Regarding the miracles of the saints, it is the Romish view that in order to be "canonized" one must perform a certain number of miracles. See Gregg Singer, "Canonization," *Baker's Dictionary of Theology*, edited by Everett F. Harrison, *et al.* (Baker Book House [1960] 1991), 109-110.

53. Reymond, *A New Systematic Theology of the Christian Faith*, 412.

As Calvin pointed out, divine authenticating miracles are those which were both *contra naturam* (contrary to the alleged laws of nature or natural order of things) and *contra peccatum* (against sin). Therefore, when Satan and his minions (such as the Roman Church-State) perform miraculous works, they are really "deceitful tricks to mislead the simple-minded and untutored."[54] They are, in the words of Warfield, "counterfeit miracles."[55]

When the organs of special revelation completed their writing of the New Testament, the authenticating credentials were no longer necessary. Hence, even though Satan and his minions may continue to deceive "the simple-minded and untutored" with their supernatural miracles, the truth of the matter is that "those former ways of God's revealing His will unto His people [have] now ceased." Once again, to assert that divine miracles still occur today is anti-Biblical.

According to the Westminster Assembly, Scripture consists of the 66 books of the Old and New Testaments. The 39 Old Testament books, which had been collected (the Palestinian Canon) prior to the coming of Christ, were validated by Christ and His apostles. The inspired writing of the 27 New Testament books was completed by the end of the first century. The canon was closed. The list of books in the canon was not officially published until 397, by the Council of Carthage. As far as we know (and such history, not being revealed in Scripture, is always subject to revision), that Council was the first to publish a list of the 27 inspired books written at least 300 years earlier and recognized as Scripture and used by Christians as Scripture for centu-

54. Calvin, *Institutes*, "Prefatory Address to King Francis I of France." See also Reymond, *A New Systematic Theology of the Christian Faith*, 409-411.

55. Benjamin B. Warfield, *Counterfeit Miracles* (The Banner of Truth Trust [1918] 1983).

ries. The complete Bible, all 66 books of both the Old and New Testaments, preceded and had been received as Scripture by churches and individual Christians for centuries before any council made a list. To suggest that the Council made the canon is to read history backwards.

In the New Testament itself we see clear evidence of the formulation of such a list. We read, for instance, of "the [apostolic] traditions" (*1 Corinthians* 11:2; *2 Thessalonians* 2:15; 3:6), "the pattern of doctrine" (*Romans* 6:17), "the pattern of sound words" (*2 Timothy* 1:13-14), "the faith once delivered to the saints" (*Jude* 3), and "the faithful sayings" of Paul's pastoral epistles (*1 Timothy* 1:15; 3:1; 4:8-9; *2 Timothy* 2:11-13; *Titus* 3:3-8).

In the early years of the church there was some difference of opinion as to which New Testament books should be recognized as authoritative. *Hebrews, James, 2 Peter, 2* and *3 John, Jude,* and *Revelation* were among the *antilegomena* ("disputed writings"). The rest of the books were considered a part of the *homologoumena* ("agreed upon" books). But according to Ridderbos and Bruce, questions regarding some of the New Testament books arose only after the Gnostic heretic Marcion (*c.* 160) made his own list of books which included only a small number of the already recognized New Testament books.[56] The Gnostics held a view similar to that of the later Roman Church-State. That is, the Gnostics averred that they had greater insight into the Scriptures than ordinary Christians; hence, they were better able to determine what was and what was not God's Word, and how that Word must be interpreted. This Gnostic tradition is part of the Roman Catholic doctrine of the Magisterium in

56. Herman N. Ridderbos, *Redemptive History and the New Testament* (Presbyterian and Reformed, 1988), 40; F. F. Bruce, *The Canon of Scripture* (InterVarsity Press, 1988), 255.

the third millennium after Christ, which claims that it alone is uniquely endowed by the Holy Spirit to discern and interpret Scripture.

The fact is that the early church never taught that it made the canon or decided what was God's Word. It recognized the 27 books as those "which are given by inspiration of God to be the rule of faith and life," and received them into the canon. In the words of Hendriksen:

> It is not because the church upon a certain date, long ago, made an official decision, that these sixty-six books constitute the inspired Bible. On the contrary, it is because God's people had long since accepted these books as being the very Word of God that the church finally made this official declaration before the world. The sixty-six books, by their very contents, immediately attest themselves to the hearts of God's children as being the living oracles of God.[57]

The Protestant view is that the church is the witness to, the recognizer of, and the servant of Scripture. That is, the church was created by, received, acknowledged, and submitted to the Scriptures (the verb the early church used was *recipimus*, "we receive"). Martin Luther used this striking analogy: "This deduction is utterly absurd: I approve Scripture; therefore, I am above it. John the Baptist approves and confesses Christ and points him out with his finger; therefore, he is above Christ! The church approves Christian doctrine and faith; therefore, she is above them." *The Chicago Statement on Biblical Inerrancy* (Articles I and II) says it this way: "We deny that the Scriptures receive their authority from the church, tradition, or any other human

---

57. Hendriksen, *Survey of the Bible*, 23.

source.... We affirm that the Scriptures are the supreme written norm by which God binds the conscience, and that the authority of the church is subordinate to that of Scripture.... We deny that church creeds, councils, or declarations have authority greater than or equal to the authority of the Bible." That statement accurately reflects the thought and action of the first Christians.

The Roman Church-State, on the other hand, like the early Gnostics, considers itself to have superior and unique spiritual insight, and therefore it is the sole determiner of, the sole interpreter of, and the custodian and master of Scripture. The present writer is well aware of the fact that some misinformed Romanists deny that the Roman Church-State makes these claims. Vatican I made a distinction between divine and human authorship that some have misinterpreted. It pronounced that the books of the Bible (including the *Apocrypha*, of course) are held by the church to be "sacred and canonical, not because, having been carefully composed by mere human industry, they were afterwards approved by her authority...but because, having been written by the inspiration of the Holy Ghost, they have God for their author, and have been delivered as such to the church herself."[58] But in Romanist doctrine this statement is quite compatible with and actually complementary to the notion that the Roman Church-State itself was the inspired author of Scripture and the only proper interpreter of Scripture. In affirming that the *Apocrypha* is Scripture, that God's Word comes in two forms, oral tradition and the Bible, and that it is the only infallible interpreter of Scripture, the Roman Church-State has unquestionably stated that it has the authority to determine and constitute

58. Schaff, "Dogmatic Decrees of the Vatican Council," Chapter II, *The Creeds of Christendom*, II:241-242.

what is and what is not the very Word of God.[59] Then, too, the *Catechism of the Catholic Church* overtly states that "it was by the apostolic tradition that the church discerned which writings are to be included in the list of the sacred books."[60]

We have already seen that Thomas Aquinas believed that by means of rational proofs he had established the divine origin of the Roman Catholic Church. With itself established by reason, the Roman Church-State can then certify the divinity of the Bible, and declare which books are Scripture. Too, the divinely established Roman Church, it is asserted, with its infallible pope, is alone able to interpret infallibly the Scriptures for us. The Roman Catholic Church, then, not the Scriptures, speaks with the supreme authority of Christ.[61] Its rule is *sola Ekklesia*, not *sola Scriptura*.

G. I. Williamson correctly stated: "The Roman Catholic Church nowhere reveals its supreme audacity more clearly than it does here. Rome says the Bible is the Word of God. But it also says that the certainty of this is dependent upon the testimony of the [Roman Catholic] Church." Williamson goes on to quote the words of a Roman Catholic textbook: "Even though these texts from Scripture are exceedingly clear, they cannot possibly

59. Grudem, *Systematic Theology: An Introduction to Biblical Doctrine*, 59.

60. *Catechism of the Catholic Church*, paragraph 120. The *Catechism* here makes much of the uncareful statement of Augustine, in his *Contra epistolam Manichaei*, 5-6: "But I would not believe in the Gospel, had not the authority of the catholic church already moved me" (paragraph 119). But as Calvin pointed out, Augustine here was referring to the fact that it is the church, by its ministerial authority, that introduces the Gospel to unbelievers (in this case the Manichees) , and not that the Gospel in any way depends upon the church (*Institutes* I:7:3). A doctrine that relies on such ambiguities is not sound doctrine.

61. Erickson, *Christian Theology*, 245-246.

be our main proof that the Bible is the inspired Word of God.... The Scripture needed a guarantee of authenticity. The [Roman Catholic] Church alone could give that guarantee; without the [Roman Catholic] Church it cannot exist."[62]

As arrogant and as impious as these words may (and should) sound, they are the official teaching of Roman Catholicism. Similar statements are found in the writings of some sixteenth century Romanists.[63] Eckius, for example, claimed that: "The Church is more ancient than the Scriptures, and that the Scripture is not authentic but by the authority of the Church.... The Church is above the Scripture." Pighius stated: "All the authority which the Scripture now has with us depends necessarily upon the authority of the Church." And Hosius wrote: "In truth, unless the authority of the Church had taught us that this was canonical Scripture, it would have very slight weight with us."

According to Rome, what the Roman Church-State says is more authoritative than what God says in His written Word. According to Romanism, God cannot guarantee His Word by His Word, but the Roman Church-State can guarantee God's Word by its word. Simply stated, this is blasphemous.

In contrast to Rome, the Christian view is well summarized by Louis Gaussen as follows:

> In this affair, then, the church is a servant and not a mistress; a depository and not a judge. She exercises the office of a minister, not of a magistrate.

---

62. G. I. Williamson, *The Westminster Confession of Faith for Study Classes* (Presbyterian and Reformed, 1980), 7-8. The textbook cited is *Catholic Theology for Laymen*; the author of the words quoted by Williamson is F. J. Ripley.

63. The quotes from the following three authors are cited in Whitaker, *A Disputation on Holy Scripture*, 276-277.

> She delivers a testimony, not a judicial sentence. She discerns the canon of the Scriptures, she does not make it; she has recognized their authenticity, she has not given it.
>
> The authority of the Scriptures is not founded, then, on the authority of the church: It is the church that is founded on the authority of the Scriptures.[64]

The churches of the first, second, third, and fourth centuries did employ certain criteria when recognizing the books of the New Testament. The criteria included apostolicity (was a given book written by an apostle or one having apostolic endorsement?), the acceptance of the apostles, and consistency of doctrine (was a given book doctrinally correct, that is, was it in accord with the balance of Biblical teaching?).

The difficulty here is that apostolic authorship alone cannot determine canonicity. Paul, for example, apparently wrote another letter which was not received as canonical (see *1 Corinthians* 5:9). And, of course, some books were written by men who were not apostles. Neither does acceptance by the early churches nor the consistency of doctrine afford canonical status. The canonicity of the Bible is in no sense subjective. The list of books is what it is solely because of the books' objective, authoritative inspiration by God the Holy Spirit.[65] Christ Himself taught that "I do not receive testimony from man" (*John* 5:34). If Christ does not depend upon the testimony or authority of man, neither does His Word, because the authority of Scripture is not less than that of Christ, Whose Word it is. As the *Confession* (1:4)

64. Louis Gaussen, *God-Breathed*, translated by David D. Scott (The Trinity Foundation [1841] 2001), 132.

65. See Richard B. Gaffin, Jr., "The New Testament as Canon," *Inerrancy and Hermeneutics*, edited by Harvey M. Conn (Baker Book House, 1988), 168-170.

says: "The authority of Holy Scripture...depends not upon the testimony of any man [such as the pope], or church [such as the Roman Catholic Church]; but wholly upon God (Who is truth itself), the author thereof; and therefore it is to be received because it is the Word of God."

It is also noteworthy that the Reformers endorsed the 66 book canon, denying that the *Apocrypha* or any other writings or church traditions were to be given Scriptural status. As we have seen, this too was the position adopted by the major confessional statements of the church throughout the sixteenth and seventeenth centuries. Again, God Himself determines the canon. Protestantism maintains that every book of the Bible was canonical at the time of its composition, due to its inspired nature. The churches merely recognized this canonical status, and received the books as God's Word centuries before a list was published by a council. The church did not establish the canon, any more than the church inspired the Scriptures.

The *Confession* affirms that all 66 of the books of the Bible "are given by inspiration of God." Charles Hodge (1797-1878) defined the orthodox view of inspiration as follows: "On this subject the common doctrine of the church is, and ever has been, that inspiration was an influence of the Holy Spirit on the minds of certain select men, which rendered them the organs of God for the infallible communication of His mind and will. They were in such a sense the organs of God, that what they said God said."[66]

The Westminster Assembly made its assertion concerning Biblical inspiration because the Bible itself claims that "all Scripture is given by inspiration of God" (*2 Timothy* 3:16). The Greek word translated as "given by inspiration" is *theopneustos*. As

66. Charles Hodge, *Systematic Theology* (Eerdmans, 1977), 1:154.

Warfield pointed out, "God-breathed out" is a better translation of the original word, because *theopneustos* actually means that Scripture is "breathed out" of the mouth of God, whereas "inspired" means "breathed in."[67]

In other words, *theopneustos* has to do, not with the transmission of Scripture, but with its origin. What Paul is saying is that the Scripture owes its origin and its content to the creative breath of God. God alone speaks in the Scriptures as the primary author. In the words of the *Confession* (1:8), the original autographs (the *autographa*) were "immediately inspired by God." This is why Jesus refers to Scripture as "the mouth of God" (*Matthew* 4:4).

While *2 Timothy* 3:16 teaches that the writings are inspired (or God-breathed), *2 Peter* 1:20-21 affirm that the same is true of the human authors, that is, at the time of their writing Scripture. The Holy Spirit enabled the prophets (and the apostles by implication) to inscribe God's revelation without error. They were "moved along" by the Spirit so that their writings were nothing other than the Word of God. Peter claims that no Biblical revelation had its origin in men's thoughts; the originator of all Scriptural revelation is God. Yet the men were used in accordance with their own personal abilities and disabilities (themselves created by God), by the Spirit, as He "moved them along" to write His Word infallibly. As stated in Article VIII of the *Chicago Statement of Biblical Inerrancy:* "We affirm that God in His work of *inspiration* utilized the distinctive personalities and literary styles of the writers whom He had chosen and prepared." Thus, God is the primary author of the Bible, and the prophets and

---

67. Benjamin B. Warfield, *The Inspiration and Authority of the Bible,* edited by Samuel G. Craig (Presbyterian and Reformed, 1948), 131-134.

apostles are authors only in a secondary sense. At no time is the church said to be inspired – only the Scriptures. And the individual writers of Scripture were "moved along" by the Holy Spirit only when they were actually writing Scripture. At no time did a pope, council, cardinal, priest, archbishop, or an episcopal bishop write one word of Scripture, or utter one word of divine oral revelation.

When we study the doctrine of Biblical inspiration we are studying the means by which special revelation is given. There is a difference between special revelation and inspiration. The former is that body of truth that we have in the Scriptures. The latter is that supernatural work of the Holy Spirit on the human authors of Scripture, whereby their words are rendered as one and the same as God's words, and therefore, inerrant and infallible. By means of inspiration, God gives us special revelation. Let us first briefly consider some erroneous views of inspiration.[68]

The *mechanical* and/or *dictation* theory maintains that the human authors were little more than stenographers, as God dictated words to them. It is true that sometimes God did dictate to the human authors, as with Moses at Mount Sinai (*Exodus* 20-23; see 24:4), but it does not follow that all Scripture was dictated in that fashion. It is obvious, for example, from *Luke* 1:1-4 that the *Gospel* writer was very active in his writing. So while parts of Scripture may have been strictly dictated by God (how else could Moses have written *Genesis* 1-3?), other parts may not have been strictly dictated; yet all are equally inspired and infallible. But the central problem with the dictation theory is not that it accords too much control to God, but too little. Unlike a businessman and his stenographer, God created and prepared

68. Compare Geisler and Nix, *A General Introduction to the Bible*, 165-190.

His stenographers in every detail of their lives (*Psalm* 139:13-16), so that their personalities and education was exactly what God required to write His Word.

The *dynamic* theory teaches that the human authors were moved by God's Spirit to a higher level of Christian life. They saw things more clearly than most men do, but the words they wrote are not actually God's words. The men may have been in some sense inspired, but certainly not their writings. They, not the Holy Spirit, chose which words to write. But this contradicts many explicit statements of Scripture in which God says that He will place His own words in the mouths of the prophets (*2 Samuel* 23:2; *Jeremiah* 1:4-10).

The *partial inspiration* theory avers that only parts of the Bible are inspired. The moral or religious teachings are God's words, but not the historical or scientific. Paul denies this in *2 Timothy* 3:16-17.

The *conceptual* theory maintains that only the concepts of Scripture are inspired, not the words themselves. This is a denial of God's statement to Jeremiah: "Behold, I have put My words in your mouth" (*Jeremiah* 1:9).

The *natural* theory teaches that the authors of Scripture were men of great genius and nothing more. Their works are not to be considered as divine in origin. The words written in the Bible are merely the words of these geniuses. Apparently Israel had several geniuses disguised as farmers, fishermen, tax collectors, and shepherds.

The *Neo-liberal* theory, or "new hermeneutic," as this theory is sometimes called, does not concern itself with the historicity of Biblical events. The only important thing is the message. The Bible is a combination of *kerygma* (that is, the core message or kernel) and myth. The job of the exegete in the "new hermeneutic" is to find the kernel of truth contained within the Bible. To do this he must "demythologize" the text. His standard of truth is contemporary thought.

The *Neo-orthodox* theory, although opposed to Liberalism and Neo-liberalism, is at the same time hostile to orthodox Christianity. Parts of the Bible may subjectively "become" the Word of God (different parts for different hearers at different times), but the Bible itself is not the Word of God in any objective sense. In this view, Jesus Christ, the Word of God incarnate, is the only true revelation of God to man. And when Scripture "reveals" Christ to the reader, then that portion of the Bible subjectively becomes the Word of God to him. According to Neo-orthodoxy, it is beneath God, Who is the transcendent "Wholly Other," to communicate the transcendental Christ through logical propositions. Thus, God acts in history and his acts are recorded in the Bible, but they remain opaque until we encounter Christ. Their meaning is a subjective encounter with Christ. Neo-orthodoxy, then, in claiming that revelation is an event, not a proposition, denies that the Bible gives us propositional revelation. Further, in Neo-orthodox theology, the Bible contains errors. It was written by sinful men and is full of logical paradoxes (as distinguished from rhetorical paradoxes) and contradictions. This is why Neo-orthodoxy is sometimes called the "Theology of Paradox."

The *linguistic philosophy* theory, emerging from the camps of Neo-liberalism and Neo-orthodoxy, is an "inadequacy of language" criticism of Scripture. This critical school denies the possibility of literal propositional revelation due to the fact that language is always unable to communicate literal truth, especially literal divine truth. Language is inadequate even on a human level; the inadequacy is greater on a transcendental level.

Hence, there can never be literal truth expressed concerning the nature of God. At best we can have figures of speech, metaphors, pointers, poetry, analogies, and myths.

In contrast to these erroneous views of Biblical inspiration is the view of Christian orthodoxy, which maintains that the Bible is the Word of God; it is absolute, objective, and literal truth. Inspiration is not partial or limited in any way. The whole of Scripture, in all its contents and parts, is "God-breathed," so that the original manuscripts are infallible (*Isaiah* 55:10-11; *John* 10:35) and inerrant (*Psalm* 19:7; *Proverbs* 30:5). And God's truth is found only in the 66 books of the Old and New Testaments. The Bible does not just give us a "naked" event (that is, history without interpretation). In Biblical revelation we have both the event and its meaning given to us in logical, propositional statements.

According to the Christian view, the omnipotent God of Scripture is fully capable of expressing Himself to man in literal and true propositions. As God's created image, man has been given the ability to hear and understand God's Word (see *Genesis* 1:28; 2:15-17). God reveals Himself in His Word. He speaks to persons in propositions, commands, and questions – all verbal. It is God Who has made man's mouth (*Exodus* 4:11), and made language the vehicle by which man is able to communicate in literal and truthful statements with God and his fellow man. Article IV of the *Chicago Statement on Biblical Inerrancy* states: "We affirm that God who has made mankind in His image has used language as a means of revelation. We deny that human language is so limited by our creatureliness that it is rendered inadequate as a vehicle for divine revelation."

The orthodox view of inspiration, sometimes called the "organic" view, avers that God has from all eternity chosen the individuals whom He would have pen His infallible Word (*Jeremiah* 1:4-10). He created and controlled the human writers, fashioning them, shaping their individual personalities, endowing them with character traits and talents (*Psalm* 139:13-16) for their task of writing. Then, in His perfect timing, God caused them to write Holy Scripture. Each human author used his own particular God-given style, and all the while it was the Holy Spirit moving him to write infallible truth (*2 Peter* 1:20-21).

In *2 Timothy* 3, Paul teaches that the whole Bible is God-breathed. Not only is this true of the "sacred writings" (*hiera grammata*) of the Old Testament (verse 15), but it is also true of "all Scripture" (*pasa graphe*), the New as well as the Old (verse 16). This is the doctrine of plenary inspiration, which maintains that the Bible is inspired in all its parts. That is, *1 Chronicles* is just as much inspired as the *Gospel of John*. The *Gospel of John* may be more satisfying and consoling to us than *1 Chronicles*, but it is not more inspired.

Plenary inspiration also directly relates to Biblical chronology. This is especially noteworthy in our day, when not only the atheistic evolutionists, theistic evolutionists, and progressive creationists, but also the so-called "old earth creationists" claim that the universe is between eight and twelve billion years old, and the Earth itself is almost five billion years old. The present day pope, John Paul II, in conformity with official Roman Catholic policy, which permits a variety of beliefs on this subject, has given his endorsement of biological evolution. Pius XII in a papal encyclical also permitted the acceptance of theistic evolution. Roman Catholicism teaches that God is the Creator of the universe and the soul of man. But beyond this, members of the

Roman Church-State are free to believe in both creation and/or evolution.[69]

The Bible, on the other hand, indicates that the cosmos was created by God in a period of six days, several thousand years ago (*Genesis* 1). If we are going to doubt the correct dates given to us in Scripture, what else are we going to doubt? Wayne Jackson accurately summarized the importance of this matter:

> The purpose of Biblical chronology is to determine the correct dates of events and persons recorded in the Bible as accurately as possible, in order that we may better understand their role in the great plan of Jehovah.
>
> The Bible is the inspired Word of God (*2 Timothy* 3:16). Its testimony is, therefore, always reliable. Whenever it speaks with reference to chronological matters, one may be sure that it is right! No chronology is thus to be trusted which contradicts plain historical/chronological data in the sacred text, or which requires a manipulation of factual Bible information (such as is frequently done by compromisers who have been romanced by the chronological absurdities of the theory of evolution).[70]

Plenary inspiration is taught throughout the Bible. In *John* 10:35, for example, Jesus refers to the Old Testament and says "Scripture cannot be broken." As Leon Morris commented, this means "that Scripture cannot be emptied of its force by being shown to be erroneous."[71] In *Romans* 3:2 Paul says that the entire

---

69. Roger E. Dickson, *The Dawn of Belief* (J. C. Choate Publications, 1997), 179; Wayne Jackson, "Resources," *Reason and Revelation* (November 1996).

70. Wayne Jackson, "The Chronology of the Old Testament in the Light of Archaeology," *Reason and Revelation* (1:37-39, October 1981), 1:37.

71. Leon Morris, *The Gospel According to John* (Eerdmans, 1971), 527.

Old Testament is "the oracles of God." And in *Luke* 24:44 Christ places the *Law of Moses*, the *Prophets*, and the *Psalms* on the same level of authority: They are all God's infallible Word.

Regarding the New Testament writings, besides *2 Timothy* 3:16 there is *1 Corinthians* 14:37, where Paul, as an apostle, claims that "the things I write to you are the commandments of the Lord." And in *2 Peter* 3:15-16, Peter refers to Paul's apostolic writings as "Scripture."

The Bible also teaches verbal inspiration. The words of Scripture themselves, along with the grammatical construction of the sentences (syntax, verb structure), the paragraphs, and the books, are the product of the creative breath of God. This is confirmed in numerous passages. One example is found in *Matthew* 22:32, where Jesus bases the doctrine of the resurrection on the tense of the verb "to be." The Father has stated "I am" (not "I was," nor "I will be") the God of Abraham, Isaac, and Jacob.

Further, in *Deuteronomy* 18:18-19 we read: "I will raise them up a prophet…and I will put *My words* in his mouth…and whosoever will not listen unto *My words* which he will speak in My name, I will require it of him." *Jeremiah* 1:9 says: "Then the Lord put forth His hand and touched my mouth. And the Lord said unto me, Behold I have put *My words* in your mouth." And in *2 Samuel* 23:2 we have: "The Spirit of the Lord spoke by me and *His word* was on my tongue." In all of these cases we learn that it was the Spirit Who guided the writers so that the very words of God were inerrantly expressed; yet the individuality of the style and expression was not suppressed. God's style is Jeremiah's and Isaiah's and Paul's.

As noted, the orthodox view of inspiration maintains that the Bible is infallible (*John* 10:35; *Isaiah* 55:10-11) and inerrant (*Psalm* 19:7; *Proverbs* 30:5). The fact that all of Scripture is "God-breathed" demands this understanding. God's Word cannot fail, and He does not inspire error. As the *Confession* (1:5) claims, the Bible is God's "infallible truth," in which we find an "entire perfection."

Infallibility refers to the fact that the Scriptures are without defect. They are unimpeachable; they cannot rationally be contradicted, violated, disregarded, or opposed. Inerrancy teaches that Scripture is free from errors. The Bible states nothing contrary to fact; it accurately and perfectly records history and science as well as theological "facts."

The similarity between infallibility and inerrancy is immediately recognizable. There is, however, a difference; it is a difference between possibility and actuality. The attribute of inerrancy maintains that Scripture does not err, whereas the attribute of infallibility states that it cannot err. Infallibility is a stronger term. Inerrancy does not presuppose infallibility, but infallibility does imply inerrancy.

The seventeenth century Lutheran theologian Quenstedt well summarized the orthodox view regarding the infallibility and inerrancy of Scripture:

> The canonical Holy Scriptures in the original text are the infallible truth and are free from every error; in other words, in the canonical sacred Scriptures there is found no lie, no falsity, no error, not even the least, whether in subject matter or expression, but in all things and all the details that are handed down in them, they are most certainly true, whether they pertain to doctrines or morals, to history or chronology, to topography or nomenclature. No ignorance, no thoughtlessness, no forgetfulness, no lapse of memory can and dare be ascribed to the amanuenses of the Holy Spirit in their penning the Sacred Writings.[72]

72. Cited in Gordon H. Clark, *The Pastoral Epistles* (The Trinity Foundation [1983] 1998), 131.

The orthodox view of inspiration also avers that Biblical revelation is propositional in nature; it teaches propositional truth.
Propositions are logical, meaningful combinations of words that
declare something. They are the meanings of declarative sentences. The truth of Scripture is not "in between," "above," or
"behind" the words, or only in the mind of the interpreter.
Neither are the words secretly symbolic, intimating some "higher"
or "deeper" truth. Rather, God's truth lies in the logical meaning
and organization of the words themselves. Neither the numer-
ologists, nor the poets, nor those who see acrostic codes in Scripture understand Scripture. God's truth comes via our understanding of Scriptural propositions according to the ordinary
rules of grammar and logic (which are present in Scripture).
Thus, the Bible does not contain logical paradoxes. "God is not
the author of confusion but of peace" (*1 Corinthians* 14:33). His
Word is not both "yes and no," but in Christ, the *Logos* of God,
it is "yes"; for Christ is the "Amen" to all of God's promises
(*2 Corinthians* 1:19-20). "Certainly no one," wrote John Calvin,
"can be more averse to [logical] paradox than I am."[73]

There are several other Biblical passages that confirm this high
view of inspiration. They teach that there is an inextricable relationship between God and His Word. In *Psalm* 138:2, for example, we read that God has "magnified His Word above all
[His] name." In other words, the Word of God is on an equal
footing with God Himself (as identified by His name). In fact,
the Word, says the psalmist, is magnified above the name of
God, because one cannot know the magnificence of God's name
(Who He is) apart from Scripture.[74]

73. John Calvin, *Selected Works of John Calvin: Tracts and Letters* (Baker
Book House, 1983), edited by Henry Beveridge and Jules Bonnet, V:330.
74. Calvin, *Commentary* on *Psalm* 138:2.

Then, too, there are *Deuteronomy* 30:20 and 32:47. The first verse teaches that God Himself is "your life," that is, apart from Him there is no genuine life (as with *Colossians* 3:4). The second verse, however, avers that it is God's Word that is "your life," the reason being that God and His Word cannot be separated. They are inextricably related. As Christ taught: "Man shall not live by bread alone, but by every word that proceeds from the mouth of God" (*Matthew* 4:4).

In the New Testament we have similar teachings. In *John* 5:22, 27 we read that the Father "has committed all judgment to the Son." But in *John* 12:48 we are told that it is Christ's Word that will stand as judge on the last day. There is no paradox here. We simply need to understand that one cannot separate the Word of God incarnate from the Word of God inscripturated. After all, Christ is the *Logos* of God Himself (*John* 1:1).

In the New Testament there are also two groups of passages that Warfield calls the "It says," "Scripture says," "God says" verses.[75] The first group (*Galatians* 3:8; *Romans* 9:17) speaks of the Scriptures as if they were God. The second group (*Matthew* 19:4-5; *Hebrews* 3:7; *Acts* 4:24-25; 13:34-35) speaks of God as if He were the Scriptures. "In the two together, God and the Scriptures are brought into such conjunction as to show that in point of directness of authority no distinction was made between them."[76]

The Authority of Scripture

1:4 The authority of the Holy Scripture, for which it ought to be believed and obeyed, depends not upon the

---

75. Warfield, *The Inspiration and Authority of the Bible*, 299-348.
76. Warfield, *The Inspiration and Authority of the Bible*, 299.

testimony of any man or church; but wholly upon God (Who is truth itself), the author thereof; and therefore it is to be received, because it is the Word of God.

1:5 We may be moved and induced by the testimony of the church to an high and reverent esteem of the Holy Scripture. And the heavenliness of the matter, the efficacy of the doctrine, the majesty of the style, the consent of all the parts, the scope of the whole (which is, to give all glory to God), the full discovery [disclosure] it makes of the only way of man's salvation, the many other incomparable excellencies, and the entire perfection thereof, are arguments whereby it does abundantly evidence itself to be the Word of God; yet notwithstanding, our full persuasion and assurance of the infallible truth and divine authority thereof, is from the inward work of the Holy Spirit bearing witness by and with the Word in our hearts.

Section 4, which originally was written against the Roman Church-State's claim to authority, begins by stating wherein the authority of the Bible does not reside. As discussed above, in contrast to the teaching of Romanism, the Westminster Assembly maintained that Biblical authority does not depend upon the testimony of any man (the popes or councils), nor does it depend upon the authority of the church (as per the claim of the Romish Church). Rather, the authority of Scripture depends solely on the fact that God, Who is "truth itself," is "the author thereof." The Reformation principle of *sola Scriptura* teaches that Scripture alone is authoritative over every area of life. Since the Bible is God's Speech, there can be no higher authority. He speaks in Scripture; thus it compels our submission to it. Scripture is self-authenticating. It carries within itself its own warrant and justification.

This necessarily rules out all other sources of authority, such as the traditions of men (as per Roman Catholicism and Greek Orthodoxy), spiritual mysticism (as per Emanuel Swedenborg [1688-1772], and Mary Baker Eddy [1821-1910] and the medieval mystics), and existential experiences (as per Neo-orthodoxy, Friedrich Schleiermacher [1768-1834], and Albrecht Ritschl [1822-1889]).[77] As the *Confession* (31:3) teaches, again in contrast to Romanism (which declares that its councils are infallible), not even the decrees of councils and synods have authority over the Scriptures; such decrees are to be followed only "if consonant to the Word of God." All doctrines and traditions are to be tested by the only authoritative standard of truth: Holy Scripture (*Isaiah* 8:20).

According to the Westminster Assembly, then, the authority vested in Scripture is derived from its unique origin: "It is the Word of God." For this reason alone "it ought to be believed and obeyed." The 66 books of the Old and New Testaments are not only the sole authority for the church of Jesus Christ, but they are also the sole authority for every area of human life. Scripture governs all things, and as we will see in Section 6, Scripture also speaks to all things. In the words of Paul, Scripture thoroughly equips us for "every good work" (2 *Timothy* 3:16-17). And, as the *Confession* goes on to say in Section 5, it is the inner testimony of the Holy Spirit ("the inward work of the Holy Spirit") which corroborates this authority.

This being the case, the church is under divine mandate to teach the whole counsel of God (*Matthew* 28:18-20; *Acts* 20:26-27), to equip the saints thoroughly to accomplish their God-ordained tasks. The propagation of the truth was the emphasis

77. Clark, *What Do Presbyterians Believe?* 12-13, 24-25.

of the Reformation as well as that of the Westminster Assembly. The *Confession*, for example, claims that it is the inner testimony of the Holy Spirit ("the inward work of the Holy Spirit") which corroborates the authority of Scripture, "bearing witness by and with the Word in our hearts" (1:5). Further, God effectually calls His elect into a saving knowledge of Christ "by His Word and Spirit" (10:1), and He continues to sanctify[78] them "by His Word and Spirit dwelling in them" (13:1).

John Calvin taught that the preaching of the Word out of the mouths of God's ministers, when properly spoken, is to be considered as nothing less than the Word coming out of the mouth of God. Said the Reformer, when the Word is Biblically preached it is a sign of the presence of God and the instrument of Christ's rule. That is, the Gospel is the sceptre for Christ's kingdom. He approaches His people through the preaching of Scripture. Moreover, it is also the means by which Christ intends the reconciliation of the whole world; that is, the restoration of all things in Christ.[79]

Sections 4 and 5 also teach us about Biblical apologetics, which may be defined as that "discipline that establishes the exclusive truth of Christianity, on the basis of the information given to us in Scripture."[80] We saw above that a consistently Biblical apologetic rejects the natural theology of Thomas Aquinas and modern day evidentialists. It does not attempt to

78. Sanctification is defined by the *Shorter Catechism* (Q. 35) as "the work of God's free grace, whereby we are renewed in the whole man after the image of God, and are enabled more and more to die unto sin, and live unto righteousness."

79. Calvin, *Commentaries* on *Isaiah* 55:11; *Isaiah* 50:2; *Hosea* 1:11; and *Isaiah* 51:16.

80. John W. Robbins, "The Apologetics of Jesus and Paul," *The Trinity Review* (May 1996), 1.

prove the existence of God, for everything exists. Biblical evangelism explains who God is, and Biblical apologetics defends the doctrine of God. And as these Sections teach, neither is it logically proper to attempt to prove that the Bible is the Word of God. The Word of God is self-evidencing, self-authenticating, self-attesting, self-validating.[81] It is the axiom, the basis of all proof and argument.

Christ, for example, when confronted by the devil in the wilderness temptation, used Scripture as His only defense; He appealed to Scripture alone (*Matthew* 4:1-11). Later in His ministry, Christ taught that even the miracle of one being raised from the dead would not be sufficient to convince anyone of the truth (*Luke* 16:14-31). Once again it was Scripture that was His sole defense: "If they do not hear *Moses* and *The Prophets*, neither will they be persuaded though one rise from the dead" (verse 31). Throughout his ministry, Christ never appealed to tradition as authoritative; he never appealed to the church as authoritative; and every time he mentioned tradition, it was only to denounce it.

As Calvin stated:

> They mock the Holy Spirit when they ask: Who can convince us that these writings came from God? Who can assure us that Scripture has come down whole and intact even to our day?
>
> Thus, the highest proof of Scripture derives in general from the fact that God in person speaks in it. The prophets and apostles do not boast either of their keenness or of anything that obtains credit for them as they speak; nor do they dwell upon rational proofs. Rather, they bring for-

81. John Calvin used the word *autopiston* when referring to the "self-authenticating" nature of Scripture (*Institutes* I:7:5).

ward God's Holy name, that by it the whole world may be brought into obedience to Him.[82]

Simply stated, there is no authority higher than God's Word (*Hebrews* 6:13; *John* 8:14). The Word of God must be our axiomatic starting point. The Bible claims to be fully inspired by God (*2 Timothy* 3:16-17), and it makes this assertion often. Why, then, do some believe this assertion while others do not? Because the Spirit produces belief in the minds of the elect. As Calvin said: "Those who are inwardly taught by the Holy Spirit acquiesce implicitly in Scripture."[83] Augustine's dictum, "I believe in order to understand,"[84] is also that of a consistent Biblical apologetic.

As noted by the *Confession*, there are numerous "evidences," both internal[85] and external, that the Bible is the Word of God. There is the witness of the church, which has borne testimony to the Bible throughout the ages; there is the testimony of Scripture itself, which refers over 3,000 times to its own inspiration; there is the spiritual subject matter of the Bible, and the effectiveness of its teaching; there is a certain majesty of its style; there is the unified aim from the beginning to the end to give glory to God, and not to man; there is the full revelation the Bible makes to the only way of man's salvation in Jesus Christ; there are "the many other incomparable excellencies" of Scripture, and its "entire perfection."[86]

82. Calvin, *Institutes* I:7:1.
83. Calvin, *Institutes* I:7:4.
84. Augustine, *Letters* 120.1; *On the Trinity* 15.2
85. Technically speaking, "internal evidences" are not evidences at all in the empirical sense; they are special revelation. Only external (extra-Biblical) evidences are actually "evidences" in the empirical sense.
86. John H. Gerstner, Douglas F. Kelly, and Philip Rollinson, *A Guide to the Westminster Confession of Faith: Commentary* (The Summertown Company, 1992), 8-13.

Then too, there is the antiquity of the Bible; there are the miracles and fulfilled prophecies (there are well over 300 Old Testament prophecies fulfilled with the coming of Christ and the New Testament age);[87] there is its logical consistency: that there are approximately 40 authors, with 20 occupations, living in 10 countries, writing over a period of 1,500 years, in three languages, and producing 66 books covering a number of subjects; yet, the Word of God never contradicts itself, despite the claims of the critics, and the assertions of some of its alleged defenders. Still, as Calvin taught, without the inner testimony of the Holy Spirit, these evidences are "vain"; they are "secondary aids to our feebleness."[88] Saving faith is produced in the minds of the elect, says the *Confession*, when the Spirit of God "bears witness by and with the Word in our hearts."

What about the theological "evidences?" Are they useful? Yes, they are. Even though they cannot and must not be used in an attempt to prove that the Bible is the Word of God (how could one possibly prove, for instance, that "Esau ran to meet [Jacob], and embraced him, and fell on his neck and kissed him, and they wept" [*Genesis* 33:4]?, or that Joseph wept when he saw his brothers in Egypt [*Genesis* 42:24]?), nevertheless, they can be used in an *ad hominem* ("to the man") fashion to refute the skeptic, and to reveal the foolishness of non-Christian systems of thought. *Ad hominem* arguments (not to be confused with

87. See J. Barton Payne, *Encyclopedia of Biblical Prophecy* (Baker Book House [1973] 1987), and E. W. Hengstenberg, *Christology of the Old Testament* (Kregel Publications, 1970). Interestingly, Augustine considered the fulfillment of prophecies to be the best internal "proof" regarding the inerrant nature of Scripture. He wrote: "For what are clearer proofs than those things, which we now see to have been foretold and fulfilled" (cited in Geisler, *What Augustine Says*, 27).

88. Calvin, *Institutes* I:8:13; compare I:7:1-5.

abusive *ad hominem* arguments) do so by adopting the point of view of the opponent for the purpose of demonstrating the logical absurdity of his view. Christ used this form of argumentation frequently in His discussions with His opponents (see, for example, *Matthew* 16:1-4; *John* 9:40-41).

Standing on the infallible revelation of God's Word, the Christian apologete can and should utilize the evidences apagogically, "to answer the fool as his folly deserves, lest he be wise in his own eyes" (*Proverbs* 26:5). Such argumentation is to be used to criticize internally the unbelievers' philosophies and theologies, revealing their inconsistencies. Wrote Gordon Clark:

> Let us use as much archaeological evidence as we can find. Let us go into great detail on *J, E, D,* and *P.* We shall discuss the presence of camels in Egypt in 2000 B.C., and the hypothetical Council of Jamnia. But our arguments will be entirely *ad hominem.* We shall show that the principles our opponents use destroy their own conclusions. The argument is *ad hominem* and elenctic. When finally the opponent is reduced to silence and we can get in a word edgewise, we present the Word of God and pray that God cause him to believe.[89]

This apagogic methodology, consisting in a series of *reductiones ad absurdum*, is the principal method available to a Biblical apologist. The reason is that even though there is common ground between believers and non-believers in that both are created in the image of God, and therefore unbelievers cannot be logically consistent with themselves, there is no common philosophical ground between Christianity and other systems of thought. That

89. *The Philosophy of Gordon H. Clark*, edited by Ronald H. Nash (Presbyterian and Reformed, 1968), 451-452.

is, there are no common propositions between Christianity and non-Christian philosophies. The *ad hominem* apagogic arguments should be used against the non-believer, who already possesses the innate idea of the God against whom he is rebelling. The arguments should be used in a fashion that will attempt to make him aware of his rebellion.

After or while demonstrating the internal incoherence of the non-Christian views, the Biblical apologete will present the truth and the internal, logical consistency of the Scriptures and the Christian philosophy revealed therein. He will show how Christianity is self-consistent, how it gives us a coherent understanding of the world, how it answers questions and solves problems that other worldviews cannot. This method is not to be considered as a proof that the Christian view is true. It is a presentation of the propositions of Scripture with the prayer that the Holy Spirit will cause the hearer to believe them. It shows that intelligibility can be maintained only by viewing all things as dependent on the God of Scripture, Who is truth itself.

The attribute of the authority of Scripture is well summarized in the words of Professor Reymond:

> [T]he authority of the Word of the self-attesting Christ of Scripture is the only ground sufficiently ultimate to justify all human truth claims, and that until His Word is acknowledged as authoritative and placed at the basis of a given human knowledge system, that system remains unjustified and no truth assertion within it can be shown to have any meaning at all.[90]

90. Robert L. Reymond, *The Justification of Knowledge* (Presbyterian and Reformed, 1976), 159.

The Sufficiency of Scripture

1:6 The whole counsel of God concerning all things necessary for His own glory, man's salvation, faith, and life, is either expressly set down in Scripture, or by good and necessary consequence may be deduced from Scripture: unto which nothing at any time is to be added, whether by new revelations of the Spirit, or traditions of men. Nevertheless, we acknowledge the inward illumination of the Spirit of God to be necessary for the saving understanding of such things as are revealed in the Word; and that there are some circumstances concerning the worship of God, and government of the church, common to human actions and societies, which are to be ordered by the light of nature, and Christian prudence, according to the general rules of the Word, which are always to be observed.

As we have already seen, according to the Westminster Assembly, the Bible alone is the Word of God, and it has a systematic monopoly on truth. As a result of the Reformation, this principle was understood and applied by colonial Americans. The Bible was their textbook for every area of life; it was "A Pandect of Profitable Laws."

However, living as we do in a benighted age, it is all too frequently stated, even by alleged Christian thinkers, that the Bible is not a textbook for science, politics, economics, and so forth. Usually what is meant by this well-worn cliché is that the Bible needs to be supplemented by other sources of truth. But as the Apostle Paul wrote in *2 Timothy* 3:16-17, the Bible is not only *a* textbook, it is *the* textbook; and all others must conform to the teachings of the Bible: "All Scripture is given by inspiration of God, and is profitable for doctrine, for reproof, for correction, for instruction in righteousness, that the man of God may be complete, thoroughly equipped for every good work."

Notice the universal terms in these two statements (Section 6 of the *Confession* and *2 Timothy* 3:16-17): "whole," "all," "nothing," "at any time," "all," "complete," "thoroughly," "every." The Bible, infallibly, and the *Westminster Confession*, in compliance with the Bible, both teach the all-sufficiency of Scripture.

According to the Reformation principle of *sola Scriptura*, neither science, nor history, nor philosophy, is needed to give knowledge. There is no multi-source theory of knowledge taught in the Word of God. As Paul clearly stated in the first two chapters of *1 Corinthians*, the wisdom of the world is foolishness, and man is not able to come to the knowledge of the truth apart from the Spirit-revealed propositions of Scripture. The Bible is sufficient for all the truth we need and all the knowledge we can have. In the Bible alone, writes Solomon, we find "the certainty of the words of truth" (*Proverbs* 22:17-21).

Certainly the concept that the Bible has a systematic monopoly on truth, as expressed in the *Confession*, is no novelty. Athanasius (296-373) wrote: "The Scriptures are sufficient for every purpose or instruction or education in the truth.... It is a manifest piece of infidelity, and incurs a just charge of arrogance, either to reject what is written, or to add anything which is not written."[91] John Wycliffe (1330-1384), sometimes known as "the morning star of the Reformation," declared: "All law, all philosophy, all logic, and all ethics are in Holy Scripture. In Holy Scripture is all truth. Every Christian ought to study this book, because it is the whole truth." Martin Luther (1483-1546) commented: "Scripture...alone is the fount of all wisdom.... Scrip-

---

91. Cited in Whitaker, *A Disputation on Holy Scripture*, 680-681.

ture alone must remain the judge and the master of all books....
Whoever does not consult Scripture will know nothing whatever.... Nothing except the divine words are to be the first principles for Christians; all human words are conclusions drawn
from them and must be brought back to them and approved by
them."[92] John Calvin wrote: "I call that knowledge...which is
delivered to us by *The Law and The Prophets.*"[93] And most im-
portantly, the Apostle Paul stated that "if anyone teaches otherwise and does not consent to wholesome words, even the words
of our Lord Jesus Christ...he is proud, knowing nothing...[he
is] *destitute of the truth*" (*1 Timothy* 6:3-5).

Once again, in this Section, the Westminster Assembly condemned the teachings of Roman Catholicism. The *Confession*
also, by implication, denounces the claims of the Charismatic
churches, the Mormons (with their *Book of Mormon*), the Christian Scientists (with Mary Baker Eddy's *Science and Health with
a Key to the Scriptures*), and all others that hold to a multi-source
theory of knowledge. When we are told that tradition is necessary to learn truth, an addition has been made to the Word of
God and *sola Scriptura* has been denied. When we are told that
prophecy, tongues, "words of knowledge," and other miraculous word-gifts are still valid in the post-apostolic age, such ad-
ditions to the written Word necessarily imply that Scripture is
inadequate and not the only source of knowledge. Or when it is
asserted that science, extra-Biblical history, or philosophy can
give us truth, then we have added to the Scriptures, and denied
the principle of *sola Scriptura*. This is why the *Confession* is most
emphatic at this point: "*nothing* at *any* time is to be added [to

92. Cited in John W. Robbins, "The Apologetics of Jesus and Paul," *The
Trinity Review* (June 1996), 4.
93. Calvin, *Commentary* on *Jeremiah* 44:1-7.

Scripture], whether by new revelations of the Spirit, or traditions of men."

According to the *Westminster Confession*, and Reformed theology in general, Christianity is defined as the teaching of the 66 books of the Old and New Testaments. But notice that the *Confession* does not restrict the teaching of the Bible to its explicit propositions. It also includes that which is implicitly taught by these propositions, that is, that which can be logically deduced from the propositions of Scripture: "The whole counsel of God…is either expressly set down in Scripture, or by good and necessary consequence may be deduced from Scripture." Therefore, by Christianity the Westminster Assembly means the body of true propositions found in the 66 books of the Old and New Testaments and all their logical implications.

When the *Confession* states that "the whole counsel of God concerning all things necessary for [God's] own glory, man's salvation, faith and life" is found in the teachings of the Bible, it asserts that Scripture not only governs all things, it also speaks to all things. The Bible teaches us about redemption, but its teachings are not exclusively redemptive. Nowhere does the Bible make any restriction on the kinds of subjects to which it infallibly and inerrantly speaks. As the *Larger Catechism* (Q. 3) says, the 66 books of the Old and New Testaments "are the only rule of faith and obedience."

The Bible is concerned with family relationships (*Ephesians* 5:22-6:4), child rearing (*Deuteronomy* 6:4-9; *Colossians* 3:21), marriage and divorce (*Genesis* 2:24; *Matthew* 19:1-12), lawful oaths and vows (*Deuteronomy* 23:21-23; *Hebrews* 6:16; *James* 5:12), and the family as the primary agency of welfare (*1 Timothy* 5:8). It also teaches about the obligation to keep the Sabbath (*Exodus* 20:8-11; *Acts* 20:7), the obligation to pay tithes and offerings

(*Malachi* 3:8-10; *Matthew* 23:23; *2 Corinthians* 8-9), employer-employee relationships (*Exodus* 21:1-11; *Ephesians* 6:5-9), private property rights (*1 Kings* 21:1-16; *Acts* 5:4), honest wages (*Proverbs* 11:1; *James* 5:1-6), the rich man's duty to the poor (*Matthew* 25:31-46), free market bargaining (*Matthew* 20:1-15), the dangers of debt (*Proverbs* 22:7; *Romans* 13:8), the morality of investment and the proper use of finances (*Matthew* 25:14-30), and the obligation of leaving an inheritance (*Proverbs* 13:22; *2 Corinthians* 12:14). Then, too, Scripture gives us laws regarding godly citizenship (*Matthew* 22:21), the proper function of the civil magistrate (*Romans* 13:1-6; *1 Peter* 2:13-17), lawsuits and court action (*Deuteronomy* 17:2-13; *1 Corinthians* 6:1-8), just penology (*Genesis* 9:5-6; *Exodus* 22:24-25), taxation (*Exodus* 30:11-16; *1 Samuel* 8:10-18), lawful warfare (*Deuteronomy* 20:1-20), and much more. The teaching of Scripture is full-scaled in nature; it thoroughly equips us "for every good work."

B. B. Warfield, commenting on this Section of the *Confession* (1:6), wrote:

> It must be observed, however, that the teachings and prescriptions of Scripture are not confined by the *Confession* to what is "expressly set down in Scripture." Men are required to believe and obey not only what is "expressly set down in Scripture," but also what "by good and necessary consequence may be deduced from Scripture." This is the strenuous and universal contention of the Reformed theology against the Socinians and Arminians, who desire to confine the authority of Scripture to its literal asseverations; and it involves a characteristic honoring of reason as the instrument for the ascertainment of truth. We must depend upon our human faculties to ascertain what Scripture says; we cannot suddenly abnegate them and refuse

their guidance in determining what Scripture *means*. This is not, of course, to make reason the ground of the authority of inferred doctrines and duties. Reason is the instrument of discovery of all doctrines and duties, whether "expressly set down in Scripture" or "by good and necessary consequence deduced from Scripture": but their authority, when once discovered, is derived from God, who reveals and prescribes them in Scripture, either by literal assertion or by necessary implication. The *Confession* is only zealous, as it declares that only Scripture is the authoritative rule of faith and practice, so to declare that the whole of Scripture is authoritative, in the whole stretch of its involved meaning. It is the Reformed contention, reflected here by the *Confession*, that the sense of Scripture is Scripture, and that men are bound by its whole sense in all its implications. The re-emergence in recent controversies of the plea that the authority of Scripture is to be confined to its expressed declarations, and that human logic is not to be trusted in divine things, is, therefore, a direct denial of a fundamental position of Reformed theology, explicitly affirmed in the *Confession*, as well as an abnegation of fundamental reason, which would not only render thinking in a system impossible, but would discredit at a stroke many of the fundamentals of the faith, such *e.g.*, as the doctrine of the Trinity, and would logically involve the denial of the authority of all doctrine whatsoever, since no single doctrine of whatever simplicity can be ascertained from Scripture except by the use of the process of the understanding. It is, therefore, an important incident that the recent plea against the use of human logic in determining doctrine has been most sharply put forward in order to justify the rejection of a doctrine which is explicitly taught, and that repeatedly, in the very letter of

Scripture; if the plea is valid at all, it destroys at once our confidence in all doctrines, no one of which is ascertained or formulated without the aid of human logic.[94]

What Warfield emphatically asserted (and agreed with) is that the Westminster divines had a high view of logic. Logic, human logic, says the *Confession* (and Warfield as well), is a necessary tool to be used in the study and exposition of the Word of God. In fact, so important was the proper use of logic to the theologians of the Westminster Assembly that they required Gospel ministers to be trained in this area prior to ordination. In the section titled "The Form of Church Government," we read that a part of the ordination examination tested "whether he [the ordinand] has skill in logic and philosophy."

Warfield is not the only one who understood the importance of logic. Another twentieth century theologian, James O. Buswell, Jr., wrote: "When we accept the laws of logic, we are not accepting laws external to God to which He must be subject, but we are accepting laws of truth which are derived from God's holy character." And centuries earlier Augustine stated: "The science of reasoning is of very great service in searching into and unraveling all sorts of questions that come up in Scripture.... The validity of logical sequences is not a thing devised by men, but it is observed and noted by them that they may be able to learn and teach it; for it exists eternally in the reason of things, and has its origin with God."[95]

What Buswell and Augustine concluded is that logic is eternal; it is not created; it "has its origins with God." Or as Gordon

94. Warfield, *The Westminster Assembly and Its Work*, 226-227.
95. Cited in Elihu Carranza, *Logic Workbook* for *Logic* by Gordon H. Clark (The Trinity Foundation, 1992), 97, 99.

Clark wrote: "Logic is fixed, universal, necessary, and irreplaceable...[because] God is a rational being, the architecture of whose mind is logic."[96]

As important as the proper use of logic is for an understanding of God and His Word, there are a number of modern day theologians and philosophers who depreciate logic. They assert first that God's logic and man's logic are different, and then teach that there is no point of contact between "divine logic" and "human logic." Sadly, this depreciation of logic does not confine itself to the camp of Neo-orthodoxy (the "Theology of Paradox"). This pervasive spirit of misology has infected even those within the (allegedly) orthodox camp. What we have here is what Ronald Nash calls "the religious revolt against logic."[97]

Contrary to this sanctimonious, irrationalist revolt against God and logic, the Biblical view of logic maintains that God is a God of knowledge (*1 Samuel* 2:3; *Romans* 16:27). Being eternally omniscient (*Psalm* 139:1-6), God is not only the source of His own knowledge, He is also the source and determiner of all truth. That which is true is true because God thinks it so. And since that which is illogical cannot be true (*1 Timothy* 6:20), it follows that God must be rational; the laws of logic are the way He thinks. There is nothing illogical about God, nothing contradictory, nothing paradoxical. God is not the author of confusion (*1 Corinthians* 14:33); He is the "Lord God of Truth" (*Psalm* 31:5).

So much does Scripture speak of God as the God of logic that in *John* 1:1 we read that Jesus Christ is the "Logic" of God: "In

96. Gordon H. Clark, "God and Logic," *The Trinity Review* (November-December 1980), edited by John W. Robbins, 4. Much of this study on the Biblical view of logic follows Dr. Clark's excellent article.

97. Ronald H. Nash, *The Word of God and the Mind of Man* (Zondervan, 1982), chapter 9.

the beginning was the *Logos*, and the *Logos* was with God, and the *Logos* was God" (the English word "logic" derives from the Greek *logos* used in this verse). *John* 1:1 emphasizes the rationality of God the Son. Logic is as eternal as God Himself because "the *Logos* is God." Hence, though we may properly distinguish between God and logic, the two must not be separated. Logic is the way God thinks and speaks.

This will give us a greater understanding of the relationship of logic and Scripture. Since Logic is God, as the Apostle John says, and since Scripture is a part of "the mind of Christ" (*1 Corinthians* 2:16), it follows that Scripture must be logical. What is said in Scripture is God's infallible and inerrant thought. It expresses the mind of God, because, as we have seen, God and His Word are one. Hence, as the *Confession* (1:5) teaches, the Bible is a logically consistent book: There is a "consent of all the parts." This is why Paul could "reason" with people "from the Scriptures" (*Acts* 17:2).

Further, logic is embedded in Scripture. The very first verse of the Bible, "In the beginning God created the heavens and the Earth," illustrates the most fundamental law of logic: the law of contradiction[98] (A is not not-A). *Genesis* 1:1 teaches that God is the creator of all things. Too, it says that He created "in the beginning." It does not teach, therefore, that God is not the creator of all things, nor does it maintain that God created all things 100 or 1,000 years after the beginning. Because it is revelation, this verse requires that the words *God, created, beginning*, and so forth, all have definite meanings. For speech to be intelligible, words must have univocal meanings. What makes

---

98. Sometimes this law pedantically is called the "law of non-contradiction."

the words meaningful and revelation and communication possible is that each word conforms to the law of contradiction.

This most fundamental law cannot be proved by something more basic. Any attempt to prove the law of contradiction would presuppose the truth of the law and therefore beg the question. Simply put, it is not possible to think, reason, or speak intelligibly (even sign language) without using the law of contradiction. As stated by Ronald Nash:

> The law of non-contradiction [that is, law of contradiction] cannot be ignored, avoided, or dismissed as mere convention. It is a true, universal, and necessary principle of human thinking, acting, and communicating. It is also a principle that functions in the mind of God. It is nonsense to suggest that God operates according to a different or higher logic than the law of non-contradiction. If God does not or might not recognize the difference between B and non-B, there is no difference between good and evil; there is no difference between God and the devil. Such is the nonsense to which pious irrationalism would drive us.[99]

In this sense, the laws of logic are axiomatic. But they are axiomatic only because they are present in the mind and Word of God. Logic, as John says, is not something external to God. Logic is God.

Also fixed in Scripture are the two other principal laws of logic: the law of identity (A is A), and the law of excluded middle (either A or not-A). The former is mentioned explicitly in *Exodus* 3:14, in the name of God itself: "I AM WHO I AM." And the law of excluded middle is found, for example, in the words

---

99. Ronald H. Nash, *Life's Ultimate Questions: An Introduction to Philosophy* (Zondervan, 1999), 207.

of Christ: "He that is not against us is for us" (*Luke* 9:50) and "He who is not with Me is against Me" (*Luke* 11:23). There is no third possibility.

Logic, then, is embedded in Scripture because Logic is God. But the laws of logic without Scripture are insufficient to provide knowledge. This is why Scripture, rather than the law of contradiction, is selected as the axiomatic starting point of Christian epistemology. Start with Scripture, and one gets logic, too. Start with the law of contradiction, and one can never get to Scripture. Similarly, God is not the axiom, because all of our knowledge of God comes from Scripture. "God," as an axiomatic concept, apart from Scripture, is merely an empty term, without content or definition. Scripture as the axiom defines God. Again, this is why the *Westminster Confession of Faith* begins with the doctrine of Scripture in chapter 1, and chapters 2-5 on the doctrine of God follow, not precede, the chapter on Scripture.

As we are taught in the Bible, man is the image and glory of God (*Genesis* 1:27; *1 Corinthians* 11:7). God "formed man of the dust of the ground, and breathed into his nostrils the breath of life; and man became a living soul" (*Genesis* 2:7). Adam became a type of soul that is superior to that of non-rational animals (*Psalm* 32:9; *2 Peter* 2:12; *Jude* 10). Man, as God's image, is a rational creature (*Colossians* 3:10). Again, this is why the Apostle Paul could spend time "reasoning" with his auditors "from the Scriptures" (*Acts* 17:2).

Moreover, because Christ is the *Logos* Who "gives light to every man who comes into the world" (*John* 1:9), we are to understand that man's logic is God's logic. In fact, *John* 1:9 denies that logic is arbitrary, conventional, or an evolutionary tool of survival (as per Friedrich Nietzsche [1844-1900], John Dewey [1859-1952], and Jean-Paul Sartre [1905-1980]). It also denies polylogism, that is, that there may be many kinds of logic in men (as taught by Marxism and multiculturalism). According to John, there is only one kind of logic in men: God's logic. The *Logos* gives to every image bearer of God the ability to think logically.

Man, then, has the capacity to think logically, to communicate with God, and to have God communicate with him. God created Adam with a mind structured in a manner similar to his own. In the Scriptures, God has given man an intelligible message in "words of truth and reason" (*Acts* 26:25). God has also given man language so that he can converse rationally with his Creator (*Exodus* 4:11). Such thought and conversation would not be possible without the laws of logic. Logic is indispensable to all (God-given) human thought and speech. This being the case, we must insist that there is no "mere human logic" as contrasted with "divine logic." Such fallacious thinking does disservice to the *Logos* of God Himself.

One might argue here that the fall of man (*Genesis* 3) rendered logic defective. But this is not the case. The noetic effects of sin indeed hinder man's ability to reason correctly (*Romans* 1:21), but this in no way implies that logic itself is defective. As stated by Clark:

> Logic, the law of contradiction, is not affected by sin. Even if everyone constantly violated the laws of logic, they would not be less true than if everyone constantly observed them. Or, to use another example, no matter how many errors in subtraction can be found on the stubs of our checkbooks, mathematics itself is unaffected.[100]

---

100. Gordon H. Clark, *A Christian View of Men and Things* (The Trinity Foundation [1952] 1998), 201.

As we have seen, the laws of logic are eternally fixed in the mind of God, and they cannot be affected by sin. They are eternally true.

John Robbins correctly stated that "there is no greater threat facing the true church of Christ at this moment than the irrationalism that now controls our entire culture.... Hedonism, the popular philosophy of America [and secular humanism] are not to be feared nearly so much as the belief that logic, 'mere human logic,' to use the religious irrationalists' own phrase, is futile," that is, that it is an untrustworthy tool for understanding the Bible.[101]

To avoid this irrationalism, which in effect denies that man is the image and glory of God, we must return to the *Logos* theology of Scripture and of the Westminster Assembly. We must insist that logic and truth are the same for man as they are for God. This is not to say that man knows as much truth as God knows. God is omniscient; He is truth itself, and that which is true is true simply because He thinks it to be so. This is not the case with man. But both know the same truth – God inherently, and man by revelation. This is necessarily the case, because God knows all truth, and unless man knows some of the truth that God knows, he knows nothing. It is essential, then, to maintain that the logic and truth of God are the logic and truth of man. God thinks logically and He commands men to do the same.

In this Section the *Confession* teaches that there is a purpose of Scripture. It also teaches that even though the non-believer may read and understand some things in Scripture, nevertheless, "we acknowledge the inward illumination of the Spirit of God to be

---

101. John W. Robbins, *The Trinity Manifesto* (The Trinity Foundation, 1978), 1.

necessary for the saving understanding of such things as are revealed in the Word."

In *2 Timothy* 3:16 the Apostle Paul gives us a four-fold purpose of Scripture. He writes that all God-breathed Scripture "is profitable for doctrine, for reproof, for correction, [and] for instruction in righteousness." As the *Shorter Catechism* (Q. 3) states: "The Scriptures principally teach what man is to believe concerning God, and what duty God requires of man." This is doctrine. As noted, Christianity is doctrine, that is, the teaching of the 66 books of the Bible. And the Christian life, in the process of sanctification, is the application of this doctrine. As man seeks to achieve his chief end of glorifying and enjoying God,[102] he does so by means of the application of Scripture.

The process of sanctification involves reproof and correction. By means of Scripture the Holy Spirit convicts the believer of sin in his life, and as the *Shorter Catechism* (Q. 87) states, causes him to repent, that is, "with grief and hatred of his sin, [to turn] from it unto God, with full purpose of, and endeavor after, new obedience." Then, by means of Bible study, the believer is instructed in righteousness, in order that he will more properly know how to "endeavor after new obedience."

In this ongoing process of the Christian life, the Bible serves as a weapon to be used in spiritual warfare (*Matthew* 4:1-10; *Ephesians* 6:17). It is a continual source of comfort and consolation (*Psalm* 119:52; *Romans* 15:4; *1 Thessalonians* 4:18), with the moral law of God serving as a pattern of life for the converted sinner. And, as taught in the *Confession* (18:2), the Spirit uses God's Word to give the Christian an assurance of his salvation; it is an "assurance of faith, founded upon the divine truth of the

102. *Westminster Shorter Catechism* (Q. 1).

promises of salvation, the inward evidence of those graces unto which these promises are made, the testimony of the Spirit of adoption witnessing with our spirits that we are the children of God."

Finally, we read in Section 6 "that there are some circumstances concerning the worship of God, and government of the church, common to human actions and societies, which are to be ordered by the light of nature, and Christian prudence, according to the general rules of the Word, which are always to be observed." Here we are taught that there is a certain liberty involved concerning some *circumstances* regarding church worship and government; they are matters *adiaphora* ("things indifferent"). But even here liberty is to be guided by "the general rules of the Word, which are always to be observed."

First, let it be stated that the Westminster Assembly is not teaching that there is any liberty regarding the way God is to be worshiped or the way the church is to be governed. That is made abundantly clear in later chapters. In chapter 21:1 we read that "the acceptable way of worshipping the true God is instituted by Himself, and so limited by His own revealed will, that He may not be worshipped according to the imaginations and devices of men, or the suggestions of Satan, under any visible representation, or any other way not prescribed in the Holy Scripture." And in chapter 30:1, we are taught that "the Lord Jesus, as King and Head of His church, has therein appointed a government, in the hand of church officers, distinct from the civil magistrate."

What the *Confession* is speaking to here, then, has to do with *circumstances*, not the ways, or the elements of worship and church government. For example, Scripture clearly teaches that we are to worship God on the Lord's Day (*Acts* 20:7; *1 Corinthians* 16:1-

2), but we are not told at what hour of the Lord's Day worship services are to be held. This is a circumstance of worship that is to be determined by the church officers. Then too, we are told that the church is to be governed by church officers. But we are not told on what day of the week or what hour of the day these officers should meet to discuss church business, to make decisions regarding the work of the church, and so forth. Christian prudence, governed "according to the general rules of the Word," is to be used in these matters. As Paul teaches: "Let all things be done decently and in order" (*1 Corinthians* 14:40).

The Clarity of Scripture

> 1:7 All things in Scripture are not alike plain in themselves, nor alike clear unto all; yet those things which are necessary to be known, believed, and observed for salvation are so clearly propounded and opened in some place of Scripture or other, that not only the learned, but the unlearned, in a due use of the ordinary means, may attain unto a sufficient understanding of them.

According to the *Confession*, not only has God revealed Himself in the 66 books of the Bible, He has done so in a manner that is clear and comprehensible. God has spoken in His Word in order to be understood. In the words of Paul: "For we do not write you anything you cannot read or understand" (*2 Corinthians* 1:13; *New International Version*).

The *Confession* does not deny that some teachings of Scripture are harder to understand than others. For instance, Peter writes: "as also in all his [Paul's] epistles, speaking in them of these things, in which are some things hard to understand" (*2 Peter* 3:16). But note that Peter does not say that "all things" or "many things" which Paul writes are "hard to understand," but only "some things." Further, the apostle does not teach us that these "some things" cannot be understood; he merely claims that "some things are hard to understand," clearly indicating that they can be understood with further study. Then too, Peter goes on to say, in the same verse, it is those who are "untaught" and "unstable" who "twist" these teachings "to their own destruction, as they do the rest of the Scriptures." As Paul wrote: "But even if our Gospel is veiled, it is veiled to those who are perishing" (*2 Corinthians* 4:3).

The *Confession* affirms what Roman Catholicism denies: That "those things which are necessary to be known, believed, and observed for salvation are so clearly propounded and opened in some place of Scripture or other, that not only the learned, but the unlearned, in a due use of the ordinary means, may attain unto a sufficient understanding of them." As the Psalmist writes: "The commandment of the Lord is pure, enlightening the eyes" (*Psalm* 19:8). And again: "Your [God's] Word is a lamp to my feet and a light to my path" (*Psalm* 119:105). Too, in *Deuteronomy* 6:4-9, when Moses tells the people of Israel that they are to teach the Scriptures "diligently" to their children, he expects the people of Israel and their children to understand the teachings of Scripture. They were not memorizing sounds the meaning of which they did not know, as many Muslims memorize the Arabic sounds of the Koran. The same is true of *John* 5:39, where Jesus enjoins us to "search the Scriptures." The supposition is that Scripture is clear enough to be searched and understood.

It is important for us to understand that when the *Confession* says that "those things which are necessary to be known, believed, and observed for salvation, are clearly propounded and opened in some place of Scripture or other," it is not referring merely to conversion and justification. In a Reformed worldview, "salvation" relates to all of life, sanctification as well as conversion. As we have seen, the Bible teaches us about redemption, but its teachings are not exclusively redemptive. As Section 6 states: "The whole counsel of God concerning all things necessary for His own glory, man's salvation, faith and life, is either expressly set down in Scripture, or by good and necessary consequence may be deduced from Scripture."

As noted, in contrast to the Christian view of the clarity of Scripture, and the privilege and obligation of every Christian to study the Bible on his own, Roman Catholicism claims that "the task of giving an authentic interpretation of the Word of God, whether in its written form or in the form of tradition, has been entrusted to the living teaching office of the church alone."[103] Hence, A. A. Hodge accurately commented: "Protestants affirm and Romanists deny: (1) that every essential article of faith and rule of practice may be clearly learned from the Scripture; and (2) that private and unlearned Christians may be safely allowed to interpret Scripture for themselves."[104]

The "due use of the ordinary means" that the *Confession* speaks of has to do with Biblical hermeneutics, which is addressed in Section 9. But basically it is a matter of reading and studying the Scriptures by applying the proper rules of logic and grammar. There is nothing mystical about reading the Bible. Contrary to Romanism's assertion, one does not need a priest, a bishop, or the pope to tell him what the Bible means. As Gordon Clark insightfully stated: "Indeed, a reading of the papal encyclicals may convince us that it is easier to understand Peter and Paul."[105]

103. *Catechism of the Catholic Church*, paragraph 85.
104. A. A. Hodge, *The Confession of Faith* (The Banner of Truth Trust [1869] 1983), 40.
105. Clark, *What Do Presbyterians Believe?* 23.

If Peter was the first and greatest pope, as Rome alleges, why do we need another and lesser pope to interpret him? Or do we need popes to interpret popes, *ad infinitum?*

This is not in any sense to undermine the importance of good teachers, but it is to deny that the popes are good teachers. According to the pastoral epistles (*1 Timothy, 2 Timothy,* and *Titus*), good teachers are very important. Indeed, men who are ordained of God for the preaching and teaching of His Word can be of great service to us, helping us to gain a better understanding of the Word. Such "pastors and teachers," writes Paul, are used by God "for the equipping of the saints for the work of ministry, for the edifying of the body of Christ" (*Ephesians* 4:11-12). But, by what chapter 1 of the *Confession* has described as "the inward work of the Holy Spirit bearing witness by and with the Word in our hearts," and "the inward illumination of the Spirit of God," and by the utilization of "the ordinary means," "not only the learned, but the unlearned" as well "may attain unto a sufficient understanding of" the Word of God. God alone has the power to engender faith, through His Word, and He alone must have the authority in illuminating Scripture for His people. As the Apostle John wrote: "But you [believers] have an anointing from the Holy One [the Holy Spirit], and you know all things…. But the anointing which you have received from Him abides in you, and you do not need that anyone teach you" (*1 John* 2:20, 27). In other words, no human interpreter, such as the pope, needs to come between the Word of God and those to whom the Word comes. As Augustine commented: "God has made the Scriptures stoop to the capacity of babes and sucklings."[106]

A study of the clarity of Scripture, as Reymond contends,

106. Cited in Whitaker, *A Disputation on Holy Scripture*, 393.

necessitates a proper understanding of the nature of Biblical truth.[107] There are two matters in particular that need to be addressed: the univocal predication of truth and the question of logical paradox.

First, Thomas Aquinas (and Roman Catholicism in general), due to his concept of *analogia entis* ("analogy of being"), taught that nothing can be predicated (said) of God and man univocally.[108] To attempt to do so, taught Thomas, would be to abnegate the difference between the Creator and His creation. Hence, when we say that God is good we do not mean the same thing as when we say that man is good. Neither do we intend an equivocal understanding of these statements, that is, an understanding that the two uses of good are entirely different. Rather, said Aquinas, we are using the term "good" in an analogical sense. But in denying univocity, Thomas eliminated that which makes analogy possible. That is, if there is no univocal element in an analogy, then it is not an analogy, but pure equivocation.

Sadly, Thomas and Roman Catholicism are not the only culprits in this area. The Reformed theologian and apologete Cornelius Van Til (1895-1987) was also insistent that human knowledge is only analogous to divine knowledge. According to Van Til, it is because of the analogical nature of Biblical revelation that man's knowledge is "at no point identical with the content of God's mind."[109] This being the case, in asserting that there is no univocal point at which our knowledge meets God's knowledge, this view, in effect, denies that we can know anything at all, for an analogy of the truth is not the truth itself. The

107. Reymond, *A New Systematic Theology of the Christian Faith*, 95-110.
108. Thomas Aquinas, *Summa Contra Gentiles*, XXXII-XXXIV.
109. This statement is found in Van Til's "Introduction" to B. B. Warfield's *The Inspiration and Authority of the Bible*, 33.

Biblical view is not that of Thomas, Roman Catholicism, and Van Til. Rather, since God knows all things, if man does not know something that God knows, he knows nothing. If knowledge is possible, then, there must of necessity be a univocal point at which man's knowledge is God's knowledge. There must be at least one proposition that both God and man know.

The Biblical view of revelation insists that man can know the truth revealed, the truth itself, and not merely an analogy of the truth. This, however, does not imply that man can have exhaustive knowledge (*Job* 11:7; *Psalm* 139:6). God alone is omniscient (*Psalm* 139:1-6) and has such knowledge (*Romans* 11:33-34; *1 Corinthians* 2:11). There are limitations on man's knowledge, not only due to sin, but also because he is a creature. Even Adam, prior to the fall, was wholly dependent on divine, propositional revelation for knowing such ordinary things as his job and the moral law.

The Biblical view of univocal predication does not deny that there is a quantitative difference between God's knowledge and man's knowledge, nor does it deny that God knows and man knows the same proposition(s) in two different ways – God inherently and man by revelation. But there is no difference in the knowledge itself. There is a coincidence between what God knows and what man knows; there is a univocal point at which man's knowledge is identical to God's knowledge. The difference, then, between God's knowledge and man's knowledge is one of degree, not of kind. God knows more and will always know more than any creature. But if all we have is an analogy of the truth, without a univocal point of understanding, then we do not have the truth itself; rather, we have ignorance.

The second issue has to do with logical paradox. There are two sorts of paradoxes: rhetorical and logical. The former may be defined as "a figure used to shed light on a topic by challenging the reason of another and thus startling him."[110] The Bible clearly contains rhetorical paradoxes (*Matthew* 5:29; *John* 11:25-26; *2 Corinthians* 6:9-10). Logical paradoxes, however, are altogether different. Here we have a situation where an assertion (or two or three assertions) is self-contradictory. It is not possible to reconcile the paradox before the bar of human reason. The hypostatic union of the divine and human natures in Jesus Christ, and God's sovereignty and man's responsibility are two examples set forth by the advocates of logical paradox.

We have already seen that Neo-orthodoxy is referred to as "the Theology of Paradox." But there are those ostensibly within the orthodox camp who also adhere to this view. J. I. Packer is one such advocate. He believes that the Bible is full of such paradoxes (he refers to them as "antinomies"). Packer wrote that these antinomies are "seemingly incompatible positions" with which we must learn to live. We are to "refuse to regard the apparent inconsistency as real."[111] Packer, of course, is one of the prime movers of the Evangelicals and Catholics Together ecumenical movement – an activity made possible by his Theology of Paradox, Mystery and Antinomy. Then there is Cornelius Van Til. He goes so far as to say that "since God is not fully comprehensible to us, we are bound to come into what seems to be contradictions in all our knowledge. Our knowledge is analogical to God's knowledge and therefore must be paradoxical."[112]

110. Kenneth S. Kantzer, "Paradox," *Evangelical Dictionary of Theology*, edited by Walter A. Elwell (Baker Book House, 1984), 826-827.

111. J. I. Packer, *Evangelism and the Sovereignty of God* (InterVarsity Press [1961] 1974), 18-21.

112. Cornelius Van Til, *The Defense of the Faith* (Presbyterian and Reformed, 1980), 44.

Then, too, as we have seen, since an analogy of the truth is not the truth, and leads only to skepticism, those who adhere to an analogous view of Biblical revelation have no reason to deny the fact of logical paradoxes in the Bible. Roman Catholicism, then, following on the heels of Thomas Aquinas, cannot escape this same erroneous position, that logical paradoxes are to be expected in the Bible.[113] Indeed, all these men and churches speak expansively of the Mysteries of the Faith.

The Bible, however, does not speak nonsense. When it uses the word "mystery," it means a secret that men can understand, once it is revealed; it does not mean paradox. God is not the author of nonsense. As Paul wrote: "God is not the author of confusion" (*1 Corinthians* 14:33); and again: the Word of God does not come to us as both "yes and no," but in Christ it is "yes." "For all the promises of God in Him are Yes, and in Him Amen, to the glory of God" (*2 Corinthians* 1:19-20). When the Word of God Himself, Jesus Christ, enjoins us to "search the Scriptures" (*John* 5:39), we are to assume that the Scriptures are clear enough that they may be searched and understood.

The Westminster Assembly, in agreement with Scripture, sees no logical paradoxes in Scripture. Dealing with the matter of God's sovereignty and man's responsibility, for example, the *Confession* (3:1, 8) states: "God from all eternity did, by the most wise and holy counsel of His own free will, freely and unchangeably ordain whatsoever comes to pass; yet so, as thereby neither is God the author of sin, nor is violence offered to the will of the creatures, nor is the liberty or contingency of second causes [that is, man's responsibility] taken away, but rather established."

113. See Geisler, *Thomas Aquinas*, 137-149.

What are we to conclude about the alleged inclusion of logical paradoxes in the Bible? Enough has been said to show the absurdity of such a notion. But due to the fact that an increasing number of so-called evangelicals are adopting this false teaching, more needs to be said. Robert Reymond poses three insuperable obstacles with which those averring such an errant view must deal:[114]

First, to claim that such and such a teaching is a paradox would require omniscience. How could anyone know that this teaching could not be reconciled before the bar of human reason? At best, he could claim that he had not been able to reconcile the two propositions. Unless he claimed omniscience, he could be confessing his own inability, not describing an attribute of Scripture.

Second, even when one claims that the contradiction is merely "apparent," he raises serious problems: "If actually non-contradictory truths can appear as contradictions and if no amount of study or reflection can remove the contradiction, there is no available means to distinguish between the 'apparent' contradiction and a real contradiction." How then would someone know whether he is embracing an actual contradiction (which if found in the Bible would demonstrate the falsity of at least part of the Scriptures) or merely a seeming contradiction?

And third, once one asserts (with Neo-orthodoxy) that truth may come in the form of irreconcilable contradictions, then "he has given up all possibility of ever detecting a real falsehood. Every time he rejects a proposition as false because it 'contradicts' the teaching of Scripture or because it is in some other way

114. Robert L. Reymond, *Preach the Word!* (Rutherford House Books, 1988), 30-31.

illogical, the proposition's sponsor only needs to contend that it only appears to contradict Scripture or to be illogical, and that his proposition is one of the terms…of one more of those paradoxes which we have acknowledged have a legitimate place in our 'little systems.'" This being the case, Christianity's uniqueness as the only true revealed religion will die the death of a thousand qualifications.[115]

The fact of the matter is that the Bible does not contain logical paradoxes. Gordon Clark correctly stated that any supposed logical paradox found in Holy Scripture is little more than a "charley-horse between the ears that can be eliminated by rational massage."[116] William Whitaker was of the same opinion; he wrote: "Some things may seem contradictory in Scripture to a man who does not consider them with sufficient attention; yet it is certain, nevertheless, that Scripture is in perfect harmony with itself."[117] The alleged logical paradoxes are the result of faulty exegesis, not God's Word. If one stumbles on this point, great will be his fall. To opt for logical paradoxes in the Word of God is to sound the death knell for all Christian theology.

What the Westminster Assembly is calling for in teaching the perspicuity of Scripture is a Christian rationality where there is no dichotomy between faith (revelation) and reason (logic). These two go hand and hand, for it is the *Logos* Who reveals and explains the truth. Christianity is rational, because Christ is Himself the Logic, Reason, and Wisdom of God incarnate (*John* 1:1;

---

115. On these points compare John W. Robbins, "Marstonian Mysticism: The Anti-Theology of George W. Marston" in *Against the World: The Trinity Review, 1978-1988* (The Trinity Foundation, 1996), 26-30.

116. Clark, *The Atonement*, 32.

117. Whitaker, *A Disputation on Holy Scripture*, 377.

1 Corinthians 1:24, 30; *Colossians* 2:3). Therefore, His Word is rational; it is devoid of logical paradoxes.[118]

The Transmission and Preservation of Scripture

> 1:8 The Old Testament in Hebrew (which was the native language of the people of God of old),[119] and the New Testament in Greek (which, at the time of the writing of it, was most generally known to the nations), being immediately inspired by God, and, by His singular care and providence, kept pure in all ages, are therefore authentic; so as, in all controversies of religion, the church is finally to appeal unto them. But, because these original tongues are not known to all the people of God, who have the right unto, and interest in the Scriptures, and are commanded, in the fear of God, to read and search them, therefore they are to be translated into the vulgar language of every nation unto which they come, that, the Word of God dwelling plentifully in all, they may worship Him in an acceptable manner; and, through patience and comfort of the Scriptures, may have hope.

According to the Westminster Assembly, only the original Biblical manuscripts (the *autographa*) were "immediately inspired by God." The Greek and Hebrew copies (the *apographa*) which we possess today are to be considered accurate, and they are the

---

118. See W. Gary Crampton, "A Call for Christian Rationality," *The Trinity Review*, June 2001.

119. There are some scholars, such as Augustine and Jerome, who were of the belief that Hebrew was the original language spoken by Adam and Eve, and the "one language" which existed prior to the confusion of the languages in the Tower of Babel incident (*Genesis* 11); see Augustine, *City of God*, 16.11; and Whitaker, *A Disputation on Holy Scripture*, 112-114.

Word of God; but in the strictest sense, only the *autographa* may be said to be inspired.

The problem is that none of the original manuscripts is extant. What we have are copies of copies. But, according to the *Confession*, although it is true that we do not possess the autographic codex (the physical documents), it is a *non sequitur* to assume that we do not have the autographic text (the words). The good copies we do have, as a whole, can and have retained the latter without the former.[120]

Biblical orthodoxy makes no assertion that no errors have crept into the text of the copies and the translations. God never claims to have inspired translators and copyists, but He did promise to keep His Word pure throughout the ages: *Isaiah* 40:8. Mistakes in the *autographa* would attribute error to God, but defects in the individual copies attribute error only to the copyists. It is only the original authors that were inspired by God to write without error (*2 Peter* 1:20-21; *Exodus* 32:15-16; *2 Samuel* 23:2; *Jeremiah* 1:9). The individual copies are to be considered the infallible and inerrant Word of God only to the degree that they reflect the original Word.

E. J. Young[121] wrote:

> If the Scripture is "God-breathed," it naturally follows that only the original is "God-breathed." If holy men of God spoke from God as they were borne by the Holy Spirit, then only what they spoke under the Spirit's bearing is inspired. It would certainly be unwarrantable to maintain that copies of what they spoke were inspired,

120. See Wilbur N. Pickering, *The Identity of the New Testament Text* (Thomas Nelson, 1977).

121. Edward J. Young, *Thy Word Is Truth* (Eerdmans, 1957), 55-56.

since these copies were not made as men were borne by the Spirit. They were therefore not "God-breathed" as was the original.

Unlike the autographs, copies are not free from error. The branch of study known as textual criticism, which really had its beginning in the sixteenth century, undertakes the careful comparison and evaluation of the copies to determine the exact, original readings. As one might imagine, textual criticism, as Clark commented, "is a very difficult and delicate procedure."[122]

Even though the Roman Church-State adds to the Old Testament canon with its inclusion of the *Apocrypha*, as far as the Christian church is concerned, there is really no controversy regarding the Old Testament. There is only one text and that is the Masoretic Text, and it consists of 39 books. Old Testament scholar Robert Dick Wilson stated that we are virtually "certain that we have substantially the same text that was in the possession of Christ and the apostles...."[123]

The real controversy concerns the New Testament (more will be said on this below). But, as we will see, this should not be. There are presently over 4,700 Greek manuscripts of the New Testament extant. There are also a number of translations of the early church, along with some 2,200 church lectionaries (Bible study material), which are based on portions of the New Testament. Then there are some 85 papyri which contain fragments of New Testament texts. There is not one other piece of literature in all of antiquity that is as well documented as the New

122. Gordon H. Clark, *Logical Criticisms of Textual Criticism* (The Trinity Foundation, 1986), 9.

123. Robert Dick Wilson, *A Scientific Investigation of the Old Testament* (Harper Brothers Publishers, 1929), 8; see also Wayne Jackson and Bert Thompson, "Questions and Answers," *Reason and Revelation* (September 1989).

Testament. John Warwick Montgomery wrote: "To be skeptical of the resultant text of the New Testament books is to allow all of classical antiquity to slip into obscurity, for no documents of the ancient period are as well attested bibliographically as the New Testament."[124] This is why the *Westminster Confession of Faith* properly distinguishes between the *autographa* and the *apographa*. Only the originals are "immediately inspired by God." But the copies of the 66 books of the Bible which we possess have "by His singular care and providence [been] kept pure in all ages, [and] are therefore authentic."

B. B. Warfield pointed out that we are not to understand the Westminster Assembly as teaching that every copy is without error, but that the genuine text has been "kept pure" in the multitude of copies. According to the *Confession*, while it is true that the pure text would not necessarily be perfectly reproduced in any one copy, it has been preserved within the whole body of documents, due to God's providential watchcare over the transmission of the Word. The doctrine of inerrancy, then, applies in the strictest sense only to the *autographa*. But it also applies to the apographa in a derivative sense, because we do have the words of the *autographa* in the *apographa*.[125]

John Owen (1616-1683), who was a contemporary of the Westminster divines, although he did not attend the Westminster Assembly, said it this way:

> The sum of what I am pleading for, as to the particular head to be vindicated, is, that as the Scriptures of the Old and New Testament were immediately and entirely given

124. Cited in Josh McDowell, *Evidence That Demands a Verdict* (Here's Life Publishers [1972] 1979), 40.

125. Warfield, *The Westminster Assembly and Its Work*, 236ff.

out by God Himself, His mind being in them represented unto us without the least interveniency [interference] of such mediums and ways as were capable of giving change or alteration to the least iota or syllable; so, by His good and merciful providential dispensation, in His love to His Word and church, His whole Word, as first given out by Him, is preserved unto us entire in the original languages; where, shining in its own beauty and lustre (as also in all translations, so far as they faithfully represent the originals), it manifests and evidences unto the consciences of men, without other foreign help or assistance, its divine original and authority.[126]

It should not surprise us that God has kept His Word pure throughout the ages, or that the present-day copies which we possess are so accurate. The Bible itself affirms the perpetuity of God's Word. *Psalm* 119 (verses 89, 152, 160), for example, declares that the Word has been founded forever; it is eternal truth which shall never fade away. *Isaiah* 40:8 states that "the Word of our God stands forever." Then too, Jesus claimed that "till Heaven and Earth pass away, one jot or one tittle will by no means pass from the Law till all is fulfilled" (*Matthew* 5:18).

In *Deuteronomy* 4:2; 12:32; and *Proverbs* 30:6, as well as *Revelation* 22:18-19, we are told that one must not add to or delete from the original Word of God. But in *Jeremiah* 36, after wicked king Jehoiakim destroyed the prophet's original document, Jeremiah was told to make another copy. And in *Deuteronomy* 17:18, we read that a copy of the law was to be made (the original was in the ark of the covenant; *Hebrews* 9:4), and given to the

126. *The Works of John Owen* (The Banner of Truth Trust, 1979), XVI:349-350.

king so that he would know how to conduct his affairs according to Biblical law. Accurate copies, then, are attested to and approved by Scripture itself.

The accuracy of transmission is also attested in the Bible. Jesus, for instance, preached from a copy of *Isaiah* 61 (see *Luke* 4:16-21), and told others to search the Scriptures (*John* 5:39). But the Scriptures of Jesus' day were surely copies of the original manuscripts. In *2 Timothy* 4:13, Paul asks that the "parchments" (obviously copies) be brought to him so that he might study the Word of God in his prison cell. He also commends the Thessalonians for searching their copies of the original Old Testament manuscripts (*Acts* 17:11). And in *Proverbs* 25:1 we read of Solomon's original "proverbs" being copied by the "men of Hezekiah"; and the copies are considered to be the Word of God.

It is also noteworthy that the frequent use of the Septuagint (the Greek translation of the Hebrew Old Testament) by the New Testament Biblical authors speaks highly, not only of the importance and general accuracy of the transmission of the text, but also of the need for translations into the "vulgar language of every nation unto which they come, that, the Word of God dwelling plentifully in all, they may worship [God] in an acceptable manner; and through patience and comfort of the Scriptures, may have hope." As the *Confession* teaches, all persons are enjoined, "in the fear of God, to read and search" the Scriptures, thus requiring that they be able to read or hear the Bible in their native tongues. This is taught in a number of passages in the Bible: *Deuteronomy* 31:11-12; *Jeremiah* 36:6-7; *Matthew* 28:18-20; *John* 5:39; and *Romans* 15:14, to list just a few. In this manner, persons of all nations would come to know the way of salvation (*John* 20:31; *Romans* 1:16-17; 10:17), and be able to protect themselves against the evil one and his minions (*Ephesians* 6:10-18).

This same principle is taught in *Nehemiah* 8, where we read of the Word of God being read in the original language by Ezra, but being translated into the language of the auditors by the Levites.[127] Further, in His earthly ministry Jesus taught the people in their native tongue (*Matthew* 5-7). His apostles and disciples did the same. On the day of Pentecost, persons from all over the world heard the Gospel preached in their own languages (*Acts* 2). And on their missionary journeys, Paul and his companions preached the Word of God in language that their auditors were able to understand (*Acts* 13-28).

Roman Catholicism, however, is so opposed to the importance of the Bible being translated into "the vulgar language of every nation" that at one time it placed the Bible itself on the *Index of Forbidden Books*.[128] In 2002, the Roman Church-State still forbids Catholics to publish vernacular editions of the Bible without its prior permission and then only with approved explanatory notes. That is, the Bible itself is still forbidden to Roman Catholics in 2002. Further, Rome declares that the Latin *Vulgate* is the only version which is authentic. That is, although Roman Catholicism does not condemn the *autographa*, the official Church position is that the *Vulgate* is the authentic text of Scripture,[129] a view that even Jerome, the translator of the *Vulgate*, denied.[130]

127. Matthew Poole, *A Commentary on the Whole Bible* (MacDonald Publishing Company, n.d.), I:895.

128. Boettner, *Roman Catholicism*, 88, 97.

129. "The Canons and Decrees of the Council of Trent," Fourth Session; see Schaff, *The Creeds of Christendom*, II:82.

130. Whitaker, *A Disputation on Holy Scripture*, 128-135.

Regarding the matter of the transmission of Scripture, Warfield concluded that the New Testament "has been transmitted to us with no, or next to no, variation; and even in the most corrupt form in which it has ever appeared, to use the oft quoted words of Richard Bently, 'the real text of the sacred writers is competently exact...nor is one article of faith or moral precept either perverted or lost...choose as awkwardly as you will, choose the worst by design, out of the whole lump.'"[131]

Yet, all copies are just that: copies. And they are to be corrected, where necessary, by the originals. We find this taught in *2 Kings* 22 and *2 Chronicles* 34 where we read of the finding of the "original" book of the law of Moses by the priest Hilkiah (*2 Chronicles* 34:14 literally reads given "by the hand of Moses"). Although the men of that day had copies of the law (which is obvious from the fact that they were carrying out the work required by the law in *2 Chronicles* 34:1-13), there were apparently certain teachings in the originals which were not found in the copies. Israel had been guilty of not doing all that God required (see verses 19-21). Thus, obedience of the people had to be governed by the Word as it was originally given "by the hand of Moses" (verses 29ff.). Therefore, the appropriate corrections were made.

The question also arises: How are we to know which translation is the most accurate? Just in the last century there have been numerous translations, including the *American Standard Version*, the *Revised Standard Version*, the *New American Standard Version*, the *New International Version*, the *New King James Version*, and the *English Standard Version*. Most of these new translations (the *New King James Version* being an exception) are based

131. Cited in McDowell, *Evidence that Demands a Verdict*, 44.

upon a Greek text of the New Testament, known as the Alexandrian Text, that differs from the Greek text underlying the *King James Version*, known as the Received Text, in over 5,000 minor ways. Most newer translations rely heavily on a handful of early Greek manuscripts (particularly two: *Codex Vaticanus* and *Codex Sinaiticus*, especially *Vaticanus*). The theory that these documents are to be favored, primarily due to their greater age, was promulgated by B. F. Westcott and F. J. A. Hort. And yet, even among these few manuscripts, there are numerous differences.

The Westcott-Hort theory further maintains that some 80 to 90 percent of Greek manuscripts, represented by the Received Text, which unlike the Alexandrian Text, are in substantial agreement, underwent a radical editing process in the fourth century. Hence, they are unreliable. Other studies, however, have shown that this is simply not the case. As a matter of fact, there is evidence to show that the Alexandrian manuscripts were the ones tampered with, and these deliberate changes are the reason that these documents are so dissimilar.[132]

Another group of New Testament scholars argues that the readings of the majority of manuscripts are to be preferred to the readings of the few older manuscripts. This is referred to as the Majority Text, the Byzantine Text, or the Traditional Text theory. The Received Text belongs to the manuscripts of the Majority Text, but it is not perfectly identical with it.

According to the Westcott-Hort theory, manuscripts are to be weighed, not numbered. After all, it is alleged, all of the Majority Text manuscripts came from one related family. Hence, the great number of them carries little weight. According to the

132. Pickering, *The Identity of the New Testament Text*, 58-62, 107-110.

Traditional Text theory, on the other hand, greater age is not nearly so important as number. First, one text being older than another in no way implies that it is superior. The older text itself could be errant. Too, the weight of textual evidence now reveals that the Majority Text manuscripts go back at least to the time of *Codex Vaticanus* and *Codex Sinaiticus*. The fact that we do not possess any early copies of the Majority Text is also easily explained: 1) the climate in Egypt, where the early Alexandrian manuscripts were found, is more arid, thus any text would last longer there; 2) the Egyptian manuscripts were probably not used, due to their corrupt nature, and therefore lasted longer, whereas the majority of manuscripts was frequently used and these manuscripts "wore out."[133]

Second, if numbers of similar manuscripts have a single ancestor, as is alleged to be the case with the Majority Text, it does not necessarily mean that the greater number carries little weight. It may well imply that the copyists of that day believed that ancestor to be the manuscript most faithful to the original. The manuscripts that are fewer in number were in all probability rejected by the copyists; their scarcity indicates their corrupt nature.[134] Further, it is not the case that the numerous manuscripts of the Majority Text have all come from one common parent. Indeed, there is strong evidence to suggest that the Majority Text documents come from numerous parts of Christendom, and are not related genealogically.[135]

Third, the churches used the Majority Text for over 1,000 years prior to the Reformation. The churches of the Reforma-

133. Pickering, *The Identity of the New Testament Text*, 124ff.; David J. Engelsma, *Modern Bible Versions* (Protestant Reformed Churches, 1988), 27.

134. Clark, *Logical Criticisms of Textual Criticism*, 13-16.

135. Engelsma, *Modern Bible Versions*, 27-28.

tion used the same text for another 350 years (and some continue to use it). If the scholars who have followed Westcott-Hort in opting for the Alexandrian Text are correct, then the church, in many cases, has been without the most authentic text of the Word of God for nearly 1,500 years. This in itself does not indicate that God has "by His singular care and providence kept pure in all ages" the New Testament text.[136]

Perhaps the place where this problem is most noticeable is at the end of the *Gospel of Mark*. The versions following the Alexandrian Text bracket verses 9-20 as not part of the original, because they are lacking in both *Codex Vaticanus* and *Codex Sinaiticus*. But most of the other Markan manuscripts contain the verses. The common theory adopted by the Alexandrian Text advocates is that somehow the ending of *Mark* was torn off the original writing and lost. Verses 9-20 which we possess today were added by a later redactor. Alexandrian Text advocates would actually have us believe (although they would not state it this way) that God was either unable or unwilling to prevent the mutilation of the text of Holy Scripture. And certainly these advocates could not say that God has providentially "kept pure" this portion of His Word "in all ages." In fact, we may go so far as to say that if *Mark* 16:9-20 is lost, then the statement of Jesus in *Matthew* 5:18 (quoted above) is erroneous.[137]

As noted, textual criticism actually began in the sixteenth century. The Reformers were very much aware of this discipline. Believing in the principle of *sola Scriptura*, they were strong advocates of the belief that God had preserved His Word in the

136. Engelsma, *Modern Bible Versions*, 32-33.
137. For a thorough study of this matter see John W. Burgon, *The Last Twelve Verses of the Gospel According to S. Mark* (Sovereign Grace Book Club, 1959).

majority of manuscripts, which manuscripts were in basic agreement. The Roman Church-State, on the other hand, used a handful of copies in which numerous variants existed in an attempt to refute the principle of *sola Scriptura*. Without an infallible Church to tell us what is and what is not the actual Word of God, said Rome, one can never be sure of the true text of Scripture. Romanism favored a few manuscripts with numerous differences, over the majority of manuscripts which were in basic agreement, whereas the Reformers, for the most part, took the opposite stand.

Therefore, textual criticism of the last century has followed Rome, not the Reformers. And it has led the church astray. We have been told that the few texts upon which the new translations are based are better than the majority of texts upon which the *King James* and the *New King James* versions are based. As the information presented in this Section has shown, however, this is not true. The Westcott-Hort theory is not to be depended upon. As Pickering wrote, it is unproved at every point.[138] What we are talking about here is no small matter. We are dealing with the Word of God. It is not enough that the translations be accurate; the Greek text underlying the translations also must be accurate. The new translations use an inaccurate Greek text preserved by the Vatican. The fact is that the Majority Text theory, which fully adheres to the doctrine of the divine providential preservation of the Scriptures, provides a superior text, and translations should be based upon it, not upon the Alexandrian Text.

Once again, as William Einwechter points out, we see how important the Reformed principle of *sola Scriptura* is: In this case having to do with our understanding of how we should

---

138. Pickering, *The Identity of the New Testament Text*, 91-92.

judge which translations are best. Here the two major doctrines are the verbal and plenary inspiration of the *autographa*, and the providential preservation of Scripture.[139] That is, God has not only "immediately inspired" the original writings, but He has also "kept pure in all ages" the *apographa* so that they "are therefore authentic."

The Interpretation of Scripture

1:9 The infallible rule of interpretation of Scripture is the Scripture itself; and, therefore, when there is a question about the true and full sense of any Scripture (which is not manifold, but one), it must be searched and known by other places that speak more clearly.

In contrast to Roman Catholicism, which teaches that only the Roman Church-State can properly interpret the Bible for its children, Christian theology teaches that all believers are to be adults in understanding, not children; they are to be involved in Bible study; and they are able to interpret Scripture correctly (*Psalm* 1:2-3; *Joshua* 1:8; *1 Corinthians* 14:20). As stated by Charles Hodge: "The Bible is a plain book. It is intelligible by the people. And they have the right, and are bound to read and interpret it for themselves; so that their faith may rest on the testimony of the Scriptures, and not on that of the church."[140]

When Paul wrote to the church at Thessalonica, it was the whole body of believers that he commanded to "test all things; hold fast what is good" (*1 Thessalonians* 5:21). The Apostle John told his readers that they were to "test the spirits" in order that

139. William O. Einwechter, *English Bible Translations: By What Standard?* (Preston-Speed Publications, 1996), 5-12, 44.
140. Hodge, *Systematic Theology*, I:183.

they would be able to discern "the spirit of truth" from "the spirit of error" (*1 John* 4:1, 6). Understanding this, the Reformers spoke of the importance of the individual's right and duty to study privately and to interpret the Scriptures. Christians have both the right and the responsibility to read and interpret the Bible for themselves. By this they would be able to "test" all teachings, and be able to discern "the spirit of truth" from the "spirit of error." As we have just studied, it is due to the fact that "all of the people of God...have [a] right unto, and interest in the Scriptures, and are commanded, in the fear of God, to read and search them," that we are to have accurate translations in "the vulgar language of every nation."

This does not mean that every believer has the right to interpret Scripture as he pleases (*2 Peter* 1:20-21). Rather, Scripture is to be interpreted according to the meaning given to it by Christ, through His Spirit (*2 Peter* 1:20-21; *1 Corinthians* 2:6-16). This is why the discipline of Biblical hermeneutics is of vital importance. Biblical, or sacred, hermeneutics is the science of or the theory of the interpretation of the Bible. The root of the word "hermeneutics" is found in *Mark* 5:41 (*methermeneuo*, "to translate") and *1 Corinthians* 12:10 (*hermeneia*, "translate" or "interpret"). Biblical hermeneutics, as a discipline, is inseparably related to exegesis. The word "exegesis" (*exegeomai; John* 1:18) means "to lead out." Proper Biblical exegesis is the "leading out" or "explaining" of Scripture the true meaning of the text, which as the *Confession* says, "is not manifold, but one." As stated by William Bridge, Romanism claims that "one Scripture has many senses..., [but] the Protestants hold that there is but one sense of a Scripture, though divers applications of it."[141] That is, although

141. Cited in Warfield, *The Westminster Assembly and Its Work*, 252.

there may be numerous implications and applications of the various propositions in Scripture, there is only one specific meaning for each proposition. Exegesis, which is the antithesis of eisegesis (that is, a reading of something into the text of Scripture), is the practice of hermeneutics, whereas hermeneutics is the theory of exegesis.

The high view of Scripture propounded by the Westminster Assembly has several implications for a proper Biblical hermeneutic. First, as Article XVIII of the *Chicago Statement on Biblical Inerrancy* claims, it binds us to the grammatical-historical method of interpretation: "We affirm that the text of Scripture is to be interpreted by grammatico-historical exegesis, taking account of its literary forms and devices." This methodology focuses on the grammatical structure of the passages of Scripture, as they were originally written, and the historical context of the writing. According to Reymond, what this means is that the exegete "must seek to put himself in the writer's linguistic, cultural, historical, and religious shoes to discover the writer's intended meaning."[142] This being so, the Biblical exegete must understand something of the structure of the original languages, bringing to bear on the text the meaning of the words and the syntactical structure of the passage. He must also understand the historical context in which the book under study was written. Questions of authorship, date, and destination of the various books are relevant in a study of Scripture. Commentaries, lexicons, and concordances are available and very helpful to students at all levels of exegetical skills.

The Reformers stressed the *sensus literalis* ("literal sense") of Biblical hermeneutics, as opposed to the medieval *quadriga*. The

142. Reymond, *A New Systematic Theology of the Christian Faith*, 49.

quadriga was a fourfold methodology of exegesis, which attempted to find in every text a literal, a moral, an allegorical, and an analogical meaning. The *sensus literalis* method maintains that the Bible is to be studied literarily, that is, "by the letter as literature." Thus, we need to know the type of literary genre being used in the various passages of the Bible, and interpret the passages according to that genre. Parables are to be studied as parables, allegories as allegories, metaphors as metaphors, history as history, systematic theology as systematic theology, and so forth. While the Biblical exegete surely maintains that the Bible is literally true, that does not mean that all parts of the Bible are true literally. For instance, some passages are true symbolically, while others are true metaphorically.[143]

Second, the Biblical view of hermeneutics set forth by the *Confession* avers that there is a harmony to all of Scripture. The Bible never contradicts itself; there is a "consent of all the parts." Therefore, again in contrast to Roman Catholicism and its errant teaching that the only infallible interpreter of Scripture is the Roman Church-State Magisterium, the *Westminster Confession* teaches that "the infallible rule of interpretation of Scripture is the Scripture itself." The Reformers referred to this primary rule as "the analogy of faith" (from Paul's statement in *Romans* 12:6). The fact that Scripture is logically consistent implies that "when there is a question about the true and full sense of any Scripture...it must be searched and known by other places that speak more clearly." There is, then, a priority given to the explicit passages, and the implicit is to be interpreted by the explicit. The metaphorical passages must be interpreted by the

---

143. R. C. Sproul, *Knowing Scripture* (InterVarsity Press, 1977), 46-56. These same teachings are found in the writings of Gordon H. Clark; see his *God's Hammer: The Bible and Its Critics* (The Trinity Foundation, 1982).

literal passages. The narrative passages must be interpreted by the didactic.

Didactic passages are those which are specifically meant to teach theological truth. They are doctrinal and systematic. Historical passages, which are narratives, must be interpreted by the didactic. For example, the *Gospels* teach us about the life of Christ and the New Testament epistles further interpret for us the significance of the things Christ did and taught. These epistles are didactic in nature. The book of *Acts*, on the other hand, is a history of the early New Testament church. The main purpose of *Acts* is not to teach doctrinal truth, but rather to give us a brief history of the workings of the apostles and the first century church. This does not mean that we are not taught by the book of *Acts*, but we must interpret the events recounted in this history book by the doctrinal teachings of the other books. Doctrine must never be built on narrative sections of the Bible alone. Neither should we build doctrine on parables and metaphors alone.

In the *Larger Catechism* (QQ. 98-99), the Westminster Assembly has given us some guidelines as to how to approach the study of the Ten Commandments, from the standpoint of a Biblical hermeneutic. First, by comparing Scripture with Scripture we find that all "the moral law is summarily comprehended in the Ten Commandments." Then, by interpreting Scripture by Scripture, we read that there are certain "rules [that] are to be observed for the right understanding of the Ten Commandments":

> First, the law is perfect, and binds everyone to full conformity in the whole man unto the righteousness thereof, and unto entire obedience forever; so as to require the utmost perfection of every duty, and to forbid the least degree of sin.

Second, that it is spiritual, and so reaches the understanding, will, affections, and all other powers of the soul; as well as words, works, and gestures.

Third, that one and the same thing, in diverse respects, is required or forbidden in several commandments.

Fourth, that as, where a duty is commanded, the contrary sin is forbidden; and, where a sin is forbidden, the contrary duty is commanded: so, where a promise is annexed, the contrary threatening is included; and, where a threatening is annexed, the contrary promise is included.

Fifth, that what God forbids, is at no time to be done; what He commands, is always our duty; and yet every particular duty is not to be done at all times.

Sixth, that under one sin or duty, all of the same kind are forbidden or commanded; together with all the causes, means, occasions, and appearances thereof, and provocations thereunto.

Seventh, that what is forbidden or commanded to ourselves, we are bound, according to our places, to endeavor that it may be avoided or performed by others, according to the duty of their places.

Eighth, that in what is commanded to others, we are bound, according to our places and callings, to be helpful to them; and to take heed of partaking with others in what is forbidden them.

And third, the Biblical exegete is to recognize that "all Scripture…is profitable for doctrine, for reproof, for correction, for instruction in righteousness…[that we] may be complete, thoroughly equipped for every good work" (2 *Timothy* 3:16-17). Further, he must recognize that these are timeless truths. In the Psalter, for example, we read that "His [God's] truth endures to all generations" (*Psalm* 100:5), and that "every one of Your [God's] righteous judgments endures forever" (*Psalm* 119:160). Paul writes: "And therefore 'it was accounted to him [Abraham] for righteousness.' Now it was not written for his [Abraham's] sake alone that it was imputed to him, but also for us. It shall be imputed to us who believe in Him who raised up Jesus our Lord from the dead" (*Romans* 4:22-24). Says the apostle: "Whatever things were written before were written for our learning" (*Romans* 15:4). And again: "For it is written in the law of Moses, 'you shall not muzzle an ox while it treads out the grain.' Is it oxen God is concerned about? Or does He say it altogether for our sakes? For our sakes, no doubt, this is written" (*1 Corinthians* 9:9-10).

Concerning this matter, Reymond correctly wrote:

> Paul's explicit assertion that the Scriptures were written for our instruction means that, while we must distinguish admonitions that are culturally conditioned, such as "greet one another with a holy kiss" (*Romans* 16:16), from those that are not so conditioned in their application, we must resist permitting the "occasional" cultural differences that exist between the New Testament world and our own to nullify all direct application of the Scripture's instruction.[144]

The Finality of Scripture

1:10 The supreme judge by which all controversies of religion are to be determined, and all decrees of councils, opinions of ancient writers, doctrines of men, and private spirits, are to be examined, and in Whose sentence we are to rest, can be no other but the Holy Spirit speaking in the Scripture.

144. Reymond, *A New Systematic Theology of the Christian Faith*, 53.

"No attribute of Scripture," writes Reymond, "is more significant than its attribute of finality, for this attribute is the Bible's response to the burning question of our day: 'What should be our final authority in all religious controversy?'"[145] The position taken by the *Confession* that the final authority "can be no other but the Holy Spirit speaking in the Scripture" denies the claim of Romanism that the Roman Church-State, with its "decrees of councils [conciliar dogma] and opinions of ancient writers [traditions] and doctrines of men [papal encyclicals]" is the final authority. It also militates against any assertion that special revelation ("private spirits") may come by any way other than the 66 books of the Bible. This, of course, precludes such books as the Koran, the *Book of Mormon*, Mary Baker Eddy's *Science and Health with a Key to the Scriptures*, and so forth.

In the words of John Murray:

> In Section ten the *Confession* is dealing with the Scripture as canon, and uses the expression "the Holy Spirit speaking in the Scripture" to remind us that Scripture is not a dead word but the living and abiding speech of the Holy Spirit. The Reformers needed to emphasize this quality of Scripture in order to offset the plea of Rome that a living voice is necessary for the faith and guidance of the church and also to meet the same argument of enthusiasts for the inner voice of the Spirit in the believer.[146]

As Murray pointed out, when the *Confession* uses the phrase "the Holy Spirit speaking in the Scripture," it is not referring to the inner testimony of the Spirit, which was studied above. Here it has to do with the fact that the Bible is a living Word. One

145. Reymond, *A New Systematic Theology of the Christian Faith*, 89.
146. John Murray, *Collected Writings* (The Banner of Truth Trust, 1976), I:16-17.

cannot separate Scripture from the Spirit, because the Spirit speaks infallibly, inerrantly, and eternally in Scripture (*2 Samuel* 23:2; *1 Corinthians* 2:6-16; *Hebrews* 3:7-11).

We are, then, in no sense to conclude that there is a distinction being drawn here between the Bible and the Spirit speaking in it. Quite the opposite is the case. When Scripture speaks it is the Holy Spirit speaking. Again, to cite Murray:

> In all our study and application of the Word of God, we must appreciate a divinely fixed coordination. It is that of the Word of God and the Spirit of God. "Where the Spirit of the Lord is, there is liberty." God has not left us to our own resources in the study of His Word. There is the never failing promise and the ever present ministry of the Holy Spirit. He is the author of the Word and it is His peculiar prerogative to illumine the Scripture and to seal its truth upon our hearts. There are the two pillars of faith and life – the whole organism of Scripture revelation and the promise of the Spirit to guide us into all the truth. The Spirit honors and seals His own Word, and the Word assures us that "if you then, being evil, know how to give good gifts unto your children, how much more shall the heavenly Father give the Holy Spirit to them who ask Him?"[147]

We have already seen that Christ Himself, in His parable of the wicked farmers, taught that He was the supreme and final revelation of God to man (*Matthew* 21:33-40). The author of *Hebrews* teaches the same thing (1:1-2), recognizing that the Son-revelation must never be separated from His revelation through His chosen vessels, the apostles, who concluded the writing of the New Testament documents (2:2-4).

147. Murray, *Collected Writings*, I:8.

The doctrine of the finality of Scripture, therefore, enjoins us to "bring every thought into captivity to the obedience of Christ" (*2 Corinthians* 10:5). We are obliged to have our minds transformed by this living Word of God (*Romans* 12:1-2). As stated by the *Larger Catechism* (Q. 3): "The Holy Scriptures of the Old and New Testaments are the Word of God, the only rule of faith and obedience." Hence, we are to understand that when the Westminster Assembly used the word "religion" in its documents, such as in Section 10, it was in no way separating the areas covered by Scripture by areas not covered. Every area of life is covered by Scripture in a genuine Reformed theology, as expressed by the Westminster Standards. The Bible is the sole criterion of truth. It is our only textbook. Everything is to be judged by it as the supreme and final standard. Martin Luther well understood the significance of the finality of Scripture as he spoke these immortal words before the Diet of Worms:

> Unless I am convinced by Scriptures and plain reason (for I do not accept the authority of popes and councils, for they have contradicted each other), my conscience is captive to the Word of God. I cannot and will not recant anything, for to go against conscience is neither right nor safe. Here I stand; may God help me. Amen.[148]

Luther was merely stating the principle of *sola Scriptura*, that his ultimate and final judge could only be and would only be the Holy Spirit speaking in the Word of God.

---

148. Cited in Sproul, *Essential Truths of the Christian Faith*, 27; see also Gerstner, Kelly, and Rollinson, *A Guide to the Westminster Confession of Faith: Commentary*, 24. Notice that the Reformation began with a rejection – not an embrace – of contradiction and those sources that are contradictory. Those who now accept paradox and contradiction have implicitly rejected the Reformation.

Conclusion

We have seen that the high view of *sola Scriptura* taught by the Westminster Assembly was held by the writers of the Bible, both the Old and New Testaments. Quotations from *Deuteronomy* 18, *2 Samuel* 23, and *Jeremiah* 1 have been adduced to show that the writers of the Old Testament claimed to speak God's words. As a matter of fact, there are some 2,600 times that the Old Testament makes such assertions of verbal inspiration.

In the New Testament, Jesus Christ and His apostles held the same view. Jesus taught that the Old Testament was of divine origin (*Matthew* 22:29-32, 43-44; *Luke* 24:24-27, 44). He averred that God's Word was unbreakable (*John* 10:35) and eternal (*Matthew* 5:17-18). According to Christ, every word of Scripture came from the mouth of God (*Matthew* 4:4; 22:31).

In His own ministry, Jesus referred to the Old Testament writings with divine authority. He cited the five books of Moses: *Genesis* (*Matthew* 19:4-5; *Mark* 10:6-8), *Exodus* (*Matthew* 22:32; *Mark* 12:26), *Leviticus* (*Matthew* 5:43; 8:4), *Numbers* (*John* 3:14), and *Deuteronomy* (*Matthew* 4:4, 7; *Mark* 12:29-30). He also referred to *1 Samuel* (*Matthew* 12:3-4), *1* and *2 Kings* (*Luke* 4:24-27), *2 Chronicles* (*Matthew* 23:35), and *Nehemiah* (*John* 6:31). Christ frequently quoted from the *Psalms* (*Matthew* 21:42; 22:44; *John* 10:34). He cited *Proverbs* (*Luke* 14:8-10; *John* 3:13), *Ezekiel* (*John* 3:10), *Daniel* (*Matthew* 24:30), *Hosea* (*Matthew* 9:13), *Jonah* (*Matthew* 12:40), *Micah* (*Matthew* 10:35), and quoted often from *Isaiah* (*Luke* 4:18-19; 8:10). Jesus treated the Old Testament narratives as historically accurate and factual. He spoke of Abel (*Luke* 11:51), Noah (*Matthew* 24:37-39), Sodom and Gomorrah (*Matthew* 10:15), Abraham (*John* 8:56), Lot (*Luke* 17:28-32), Solomon (*Luke* 11:31), Elijah and Elisha (*Luke* 4:25-27), and Jonah

(*Matthew* 12:39-41), as historical figures and events, thus authenticating the Bible's trustworthy nature. When Christ was tempted in the wilderness by Satan, three times He stated "it is written" to express His belief in the unchangeable character of the Word of God (*Matthew* 4:1-11). On a number of occasions He spoke of Himself as the fulfillment of Old Testament prophecy (*Matthew* 11:10; *Mark* 9:12-13; 14:21; *Luke* 4:21; 18:31-33). And at other times Jesus taught that Old Testament prophecies would be fulfilled (*Matthew* 5:17-18; *Luke* 24:24-27, 44). Moreover, in *John* 6:63, Christ declared that His words were "Spirit and life." He was equating His teaching with that of the Old Testament. The Word of God was Christ's authority, and He constantly submitted Himself and His actions to the Scriptures (*Mark* 14:17-21; *Luke* 4:18-19; *John* 5:39; 13:18).

Burrell said of Christ's doctrine of Scripture:

> One thing is clear: when Jesus referred to the Scriptures as written by men under the influence of the Spirit, He separated those Scriptures generically from all other literature whatsoever. To His mind, the inspiration of these writings was a singular sort of inspiration, which produced a singular book. In His teaching it is represented as the one book having authority.[149]

The apostolic writers were in perfect agreement with their Lord. Paul (*Romans* 3:2), Luke (*Acts* 7:38), the author of *Hebrews* (5:12), and Peter (*1 Peter* 4:11), for example, refer to the Old Testament writings as the "oracles" of God, a term which attributes divine origin to them (compare *Proverbs* 30:1; 31:1; *Isaiah* 13:1; 15:1; *Nahum* 1:1, with the Hebrew equivalent for "oracles").

---

149. Cited in Louis Berkhof, *Introduction to Systematic Theology* (Baker Book House [1932] 1986), 157.

Further, Paul (*1 Corinthians* 2:13; 14:37; *1 Thessalonians* 2:13), Peter (*2 Peter* 3:1-2), and John (*Revelation* 1:1-3; 22:18-19), all considered themselves to be the (human) authors of divine revelation. As we have seen, in *2 Timothy* 3:16 Paul declares that all Scripture is God-breathed truth. In *Acts* 24:14 he claims that he believes "all things which are written in *The Law* and in *The Prophets* [the Old Testament]." In *1 Timothy* 5:18, he quotes Jesus' statement of *Luke* 10:7, calling it Scripture. And in his second epistle, Peter equates Paul's writings with the Old Testament Scriptures (*2 Peter* 3:15-16). Then when Paul (*1 Thessalonians* 5:27; *Colossians* 4:16; *1 Timothy* 4:13), and John (*Revelation* 1:3), in their apostolic authority, demand that the churches read their (apostolic) writings while in public assembly, the implication is that these writings were to be treated as the very Word of God.

Moreover, in their apostolic writings these men frequently witness to the truthfulness of Old Testament historical narratives. The New Testament writings tell us, for example, that Adam fell (*Romans* 5:12); that Abel was murdered by Cain (*1 John* 3:12); that Abraham believed God's Word and received the promise prior to his circumcision, when he was about 100 years old (*Romans* 4:10, 19); that before Rebekah's children were born God said that the elder would serve the younger (*Romans* 9:10-12); that Elijah spoke with God (*Romans* 11:2-4); that even though the people of Israel passed through the Red Sea and were spiritually nourished by Christ, who followed them, yet they rebelled against God (*1 Corinthians* 10:1-11); that Abraham met Melchizedek and paid him a tithe (*Hebrews* 7:1-2); that Moses sprinkled the people of Israel and the tabernacle vessels with blood and water (*Hebrews* 9:19-21); that Esau sold his birthright to Jacob for a single meal, then later sought it back (*Hebrews* 12:16-17); that Rahab received the spies and sent them out another way (*James* 2:25); that eight persons were saved in the ark (*1 Peter* 3:20; *2 Peter* 2:5); that God destroyed Sodom and Gomorrah, but saved Lot (*2 Peter* 2:6-7); and that Balaam's donkey spoke (*2 Peter* 2:16).[150]

The true church of Christ has held this high view of Scripture through the centuries.[151] Clement of Rome (first century), taught that "the sacred Scriptures...are the true utterances of the Holy Spirit." Justin Martyr (second century) held that the Scriptures, being the Word of the *Logos* Himself, are of undisputed authority, whereas the teachings which came after the close of the canon are not to be so considered. He wrote: "When you hear the words of the prophets spoken as though in their own persons, you are not to think that they are uttered [only] by the inspired men themselves, but by the Divine Word Who moves them." Irenaeus (second century) claimed that the writers of Scripture "were filled with perfect knowledge on every subject [about which they wrote], for they were spoken by the Word of God [Christ] and His Spirit." He also stated: "It is by no other that we have gained the knowledge of the economy of our salvation than by those [the apostles of Christ], by whom the Gospel reached us; which Gospel they then preached, and afterwards by the will of God delivered to us in the Scriptures, to be the bases and pillar of our faith." Tertullian (second and third centuries) is another who strongly distinguished between the canonical writings and all those which came afterwards. Only Scripture (not tradition) is of absolute authority. He wrote: "What man of balanced mind

---

150. Grudem, *Systematic Theology: An Introduction to Biblical Doctrine*, 94.

151. The citations below are from Harold Lindsell, *The Battle for the Bible* (Zondervan, 1976), 47ff., and from Whitaker, *A Disputation on Holy Scripture*, 669-704.

can believe that those whom the Lord gave to the church as its masters [the human authors of Scripture] were left in ignorance on any matter [on which they wrote] whatsoever?" Cyprian (third century) refers to the canonical books as "Divine Scripture," "Divine commands," "Scriptures from Heaven," "precepts of the Divine law," and "voices of the Lord." Origen (third century) claimed: "The sacred volumes are fully inspired by the Holy Spirit, and there is no passage either in the Law or the Gospel, or the writings of an apostle, which does not proceed from the inspired source of divine truth." He also wrote: "It is necessary for us to cite the testimony of the Holy Scriptures. For our opinions and discourses have no credit, unless confirmed by their witness." Athanasius (fourth century), much to the chagrin of Romanism, asserted that "the Holy Scripture is mightier than all synods.... The whole of our Scriptures, the Old and the New Testaments, is profitable for instruction as it is written." Athanasius also wrote: "The Scriptures are sufficient for every purpose of instruction or education in the truth.... It is a manifest piece of infidelity, and incurs a just charge of arrogance, either to reject what is written, or to add anything which is not written." Gregory of Nazianzus (fourth century) said: "We trace the accuracy of the Spirit in detail to each separate stroke and letter; for it is blasphemous to suppose that exact pains were bestowed by the compilers of the books [of Scripture], or even the smallest letters, without design." His brother, Basil the Great (fourth century), said that "no single syllable of the sacred writings is to be neglected." And again, said Basil, contrary to the Romish doctrine of an infallible church, "every word or action must be accepted on the testimony of inspired Scripture." Jerome (fourth and fifth centuries), who produced the Latin *Vulgate*, the official Bible of the Roman Church-State, taught that "every phrase or syllable or point in Holy Scripture is full of meaning." To Jerome, the Scriptures are the "most sure fount" from which we are to derive knowledge, because they are "written and edited by the Holy Spirit." Note that Jerome made these statements about the 66 books of the Bible alone, even though he had included the *Apocrypha* in the *Vulgate* (even while denying that it was a part of the canon). Augustine (fourth and fifth centuries) said: "The faith will totter if the authority of the Holy Scriptures loses its hold on men. We must surrender ourselves to the authority of Holy Scripture, for it can neither mislead nor be misled." He also wrote: "I have learned to ascribe to those books which are of canonical rank, and only to them, such reverence and honor, that I firmly believe that no single error due to the author is found in any one of them." And again: "God designed to lay a foundation against insidious errors in the Scriptures, against which no man dares to speak who desires to seem a Christian in any sense."

The early church clearly had a high view of the Word of God. Roman Catholics would make much of the fact that many of the early church theologians also spoke highly of tradition.[152] And so they did; perhaps too highly. But it is abundantly clear that, for the most part, the view they held of tradition was not the same as the Roman Church-State holds. The early church theologians clearly distinguished between the 66 books of the sacred canon and all teaching that came afterwards. They certainly taught that Christ's agents of New Testament revelation were under the inspiration of the Spirit, whereas later writers were not.[153] Even Augustine, who perhaps gave too high a sta-

152. Joseph Gallegos, in *Not By Faith Alone*, chapter 8.
153. See Grudem, *Systematic Theology: An Introduction to Biblical Doctrine*, 66; he cites, just as one example, the words of Ignatius of Antioch (*c.* 110), who said "I do not order you as did Peter and Paul; they were apostles."

tus to the *Apocrypha,* spoke with less reverence of these books than the 66 books of the canon. He seemed to consider the *Apocrypha,* at best, as deuterocanonical. And later, in his *Retractions,* he apparently moved even further away from his earlier view.[154]

The Reformers were of the same opinion as the early church theologians, although more consistent, to be sure. For them Scripture, not the church, was *vox dei:* "the voice of God." Martin Luther taught that "the Scriptures have never erred," "the Scriptures cannot err," "it is certain that Scripture cannot disagree with itself," "it is impossible that Scripture should contradict itself," and "it is established by God's Word that God does not lie, nor does His Word lie."[155]

John Calvin, vigorously and boldly opposing the dogma of Romanism, said:

> Between the apostles and their successors, however, there is, as I have stated, this difference: That the apostles were the certain and authentic scribes of the Holy Spirit, and therefore, their writings are to be received as the oracles of God; but succeeding ministers have no other office than to teach what is revealed and recorded in the sacred Scriptures.[156]

The seventeenth-century Puritan John Owen stated that "God has gathered up into the Scripture all divine revelations given out by Himself from the beginning of the world, and all that ever shall be to the end thereof.... The Scripture is now become the only external means of divine supernatural illumination,

---

154. Augustine, *City of God* 17.20; *Retractions* 1.30; 2.4; see Geisler, *What Augustine Says,* 48; and Whitaker, *A Disputation on Holy Scripture,* 45-49.
155. Lindsell, *The Battle for the Bible,* 57.
156. Calvin, *Institutes* IV:8:6.

because it is the only repository of all divine supernatural revelation."[157]

The eighteenth-century Puritan Jonathan Edwards (1703-1758) considered the human authors of Scripture to be "God's penmen." He wrote:

> Moses was so intimately conversant with God and so continually under the divine conduct, it can't be thought that when he wrote the history of the creation and fall of man, and the history of the church from the creation, that he should not be under the divine direction in such an affair. Doubtless he wrote by God's direction, as we are informed that he wrote the law and the history of the Jewish church.
>
> God took this care with respect to the books of the Old Testament, that no books should be received by the Jewish church and delivered down in the canon of the Old Testament but what was His Word and owned by Christ. We may therefore conclude that He would still take the same care of His church with respect to the New Testament.[158]

Nineteenth-century theologian Charles Hodge (1797-1878) wrote that "the Scriptures of the Old and New Testaments are the Word of God, written under the inspiration of the Holy Spirit, and are therefore infallible, and of divine authority in all things pertaining to faith and practice, and consequently free from all error whether of doctrine, fact, or precept."[159]

And twentieth-century scholar Gordon Clark declared: "The Bible is the Word of God...; it cannot contain error for the

157. John Owen, *The Works of John Owen*, IV:11-12.
158. Cited in John H. Gerstner, *The Rational Biblical Theology of Jonathan Edwards* (Ligonier Ministries, 1991), I:146.
159. Charles Hodge, *Systematic Theology*, I:152.

simple reason that God cannot lie. Conversely, if the Bible contains errors, it cannot, certainly not in its entirety, be the Word of God." And again, in agreement with the Evangelical Theological Society, he stated: "The Bible alone, and the Bible in its entirety, is the Word of God written, and therefore inerrant in the autographs."[160]

It is simply beyond reasonable doubt that the view of Scripture taught by the Westminster Assembly is the view that has been adhered to by the Christian church through the centuries. Interestingly, even some of the staunchest opponents of this *sola Scriptura* view admit as much. Kirsopp Lake, a radical opponent of the view of the Westminster Assembly (which he calls the "fundamentalist" view), is one such example. Wrote Lake:

> It is a mistake often made by educated persons who happen to have but a little knowledge of historical theology, to suppose that fundamentalism is a strange form of thought. It is nothing of the kind; it is the partial and uneducated survival of a theology which was once universally held by all Christians. How many were there, for instance, in Christian churches in the eighteenth century who doubted the infallible inspiration of all Scripture? A few, perhaps, but very few. No, the fundamentalist may be wrong; I think that he is. But it is we who have departed from the tradition, not he, and I am sorry for the fate of anyone who tries to argue with a fundamentalist on the basis of authority. The Bible and the *corpus theologicum* of the church is on the fundamentalist side.[161]

160. Gordon H. Clark, *God's Hammer* (The Trinity Foundation, 1982), 52.
161. Kirsopp Lake, *The Religion of Yesterday and Tomorrow* (Houghton Publishing Company, 1926), 61.

Part Two

Sola Scriptura *versus* Sola Ekklesia

Part Two

Sola Scriptura *versus* Sola Ekklesia

As STATED in the Introduction, the second part of this book intends, by applying what we have studied in the first part, to do the work of apologetics, interacting with the Roman Church-State's allegation that the Reformed principle of *sola Scriptura* is false. Many Romanist arguments are set forth by the contributors of *Not By Scripture Alone: A Catholic Critique of the Protestant Doctrine of Sola Scriptura.*[1] This principle is at the heart of the controversy between Rome and Protestantism, for it is a first principle.

As Augustine pointed out centuries ago, all systems have axioms, which cannot be proved. They are starting points, without which no system could get started. All our beliefs are ultimately based on presuppositions.[2] The Protestant axiom, as taught by the Westminster Assembly and Reformed Protestantism, is that the Bible and the Bible alone is the Word of God, and it has a systematic monopoly on truth. The Roman Church-State demurs. Peter Kreeft, formerly a Christian Reformed teacher, in his Foreword to Sungenis' book, said it this way:

1. Robert A. Sungenis, *et al.*, *Not By Scripture Alone: A Catholic Critique of the Protestant Doctrine of Sola Scriptura*. The pagination found in the text of part two is from this book.
2. Augustine, *Letters* 120.1; *On the Trinity* 15.2. This is what Augustine meant when he stated, "If you will not believe, you will not understand" (from *Isaiah* 7:9 in the *Septuagint*).

> There are many disagreements between Catholics and
> Protestants – about the nature and number of the sacra-
> ments, about the nature and authority of the Church, about
> the Pope, about saints, about Mary, about Purgatory, about
> Justification, about the Mass, about transubstantiation – a
> long list. Yet all of these disagreements are derived from a
> single one…. Protestants accept, and Catholics deny, the
> principle of *sola Scriptura* – the idea that only Scripture is
> infallible divine revelation (xv).

The issue is clear. If the Protestant church in any sense moves
away from the starting point of *sola Scriptura*, it will deny Protestantism as a whole. It will violate the apologetical prescript
taught by Solomon of not "answering a fool according to his
folly, lest you be like him" (*Proverbs* 26:4). Rather, a consistent
approach to Biblical apologetics is to stand on the rock foundation of the Word of God and "answer a fool as his folly deserves,
lest he be wise in his own eyes" (*Proverbs* 26:5). This will be the
direction of part two.

Totalitarians See Christian Freedom as Anarchy

Patrick Madrid, "the editor-and-chief of *Envoy* Magazine, a
journal of [Roman] Catholic apologetics and evangelization"
(vi), wrote chapter 1, calling *sola Scriptura* "A Blueprint for Anarchy." In it he contends that his contribution intends to give us
a "macro" look at some of the issues at stake – issues that will be
more fully dealt with in later chapters (2). In fact, Appendix 3 of
Not By Scripture Alone records two written debates on the subject of "*Sola Scriptura*" between Madrid and Douglas Jones, the
editor-in-chief of the magazine *Credenda-Agenda*.[3] In this Ap-

---

3. Robert Sungenis, the editor of *Not By Scripture Alone,* is very much of
the opinion that Madrid "got the better" of the exchange in these debates.

pendix Madrid himself expatiates on that which is studied in "macro" in chapter 1. These things being so, more will be written on this chapter than later ones.

Mr. Madrid challenges the Protestant church "to prove *sola Scriptura* from the Bible" (2), assuring us that it cannot be done. "Scripture alone," he asserts, "apart from the [Roman Catholic] Church and Tradition, is not sufficient" (3), the reason being that "there is no way, under the *sola Scriptura* rubric, to know with certainty who's [sic] interpretation of Scripture is correct and whose is unbiblical [sic]" (3). What is necessary is the infallible interpretation of the Roman Church-State. "Scripture is not always clear in all places"; yet, we are told, "millions of ordinary Christian believers [sic]⁴ over the centuries have found the Real Presence of Christ in the Eucharist there [in Scripture], they found baptismal regeneration there, they found the authority of the Church and the primacy of Peter there. The Church Fathers certainly found the Mass, the sacraments, and the necessity of Sacred Tradition there" (3).

How shall we respond? First, as we have seen, the principle of *sola Scriptura* cannot be proved. It is an axiom. The demand that an axiom be proved is itself an irrational demand. And, as we

---

This is obvious from his running commentary in the Appendix. The present writer does not share that view. Mr. Jones made several blunders in the debates, giving too much away, but all in all I think he held his ground against the Romanist position.

4. The Reformed church does not consider the Roman Church-State to be a church of "Christian believers." As Calvin taught, there may indeed by some members of the Roman Church-State who are true believers, but Romanism itself is not a Christian system (*Institutes* IV:3:12). It bears none of the marks of the church. This is also the teaching of the *Westminster Confession of Faith* (25:6): The church of Rome, with its pope, is anti-Christian, and the pope himself is the Antichrist.

have also explained in part one, the Bible does indeed claim for itself a systematic monopoly on truth. In other words, the Bible does teach *sola Scriptura*.

Jesus Christ defines truth in terms of the Bible in *John* 17:17: "Your Word is truth." Note that Christ uses the noun *aletheia* ("truth"), rather than the adjective *alethes* ("true"). Not only is the Bible true, according to Christ, it is "truth." The Apostle Paul, in *2 Timothy* 3:15-17 restricts knowledge to the completed canon of the 66 books of the Old and New Testaments. Not only the "sacred writings" (*hiera grammata*) of the Old Testament (verse 15), but "all Scripture" (*pasa graphe*), both the Old and the New is God-breathed (verse 16), and thoroughly equips us for "every good work" (verse 17). Thus, if knowledge were available to us outside of Scripture, Paul's statement would be false and misleading.

In *Acts* 17:11, Paul commended the church at Thessalonica "because they searched the Scriptures daily to find out whether these things [which Paul was teaching] were so." Scripture, not church tradition nor even apostolic teaching, still less the alleged Magisterium of the Roman Church-State, was the final court of appeal. In *Acts* 20:26-27, 32, Paul teaches that "the whole counsel of God" is found in the Word of God. And in *1 Corinthians* 4:6 he commands the church at Corinth to put their trust solely in Scripture, and not their earthly teachers. The believers at Corinth must learn "not to think beyond what is written [in Scripture]." As John MacArthur commented: "What is certain is that all that is necessary is Scripture – and we are forbidden to exceed what is written."[5]

5. John MacArthur, in *Sola Scriptura! The Protestant Position on the Bible*, edited by Don Kistler (Soli Deo Gloria Publications, 1995), 167.

In *Romans* 2:20, Paul claims that "the form of knowledge and truth" is found "in the law." In *Romans* 4:3, to settle the matter of justification by grace through faith alone, the apostle appeals to Scripture: "For what does the Scripture say?" Perhaps this is one reason why Romanism needs its church tradition to deny this fundamental Bible teaching. The Council of Trent decreed that "if any one says, that by faith alone the impious are justified, in such wise to mean, that nothing else is required to co-operate in order to the obtaining the grace of justification...let him be anathema."[6] This is why it is strange to read in the "Editor's Preface" of *Not By Scripture Alone* that Protestants, even in their criticisms of the Roman Church-State, are "our brethren" (xxi). How can those who are anathematized be "our brethren"? We need, then, to keep in mind that this is no intramural debate. If either view on this subject is correct, then the other view is Antichristian. The views are mutually exclusive.

Finally, in *Acts* 15 we read about the Jerusalem council. When the apostles and elders met to discuss and make a judgment concerning the theological matter of circumcision and its necessity with regard to salvation, their appeal was made to Scripture alone (*Amos* 9:11-12), and not to the tradition of the Church Magisterium. Hence, to claim that *sola Scriptura* is "unbiblical" and "epistemologically unviable" (2-3) is simply an extreme example of question begging. *Sola Scriptura* is assumed and taught throughout the Bible.[7]

Second, when Madrid claims that without the infallible interpretation of the church, one can never know "who's [*sic*] in-

6. "The Canons and Decrees of the Council of Trent," Canon IX; Schaff, *The Creeds of Christendom*, II:112.

7. The reader may want to look back at part one for further Biblical teachings of *sola Scriptura*.

terpretation of Scripture is correct and whose is unbiblical," he obviously denies the Holy Spirit to the ordinary Christian. Make no mistake: The Roman Church-State claims that it alone is the infallible interpreter of Scripture because it alone is guided by the Holy Spirit. But the Holy Spirit wrote and speaks through Scripture, and He guides every Christian, not just alleged bishops. Both Romanism and Christianity claim the Holy Spirit is the guarantor of infallibility. Rome says it is the Holy Spirit speaking through the Roman Church-State alone; Christianity says it is the Holy Spirit speaking through Scripture alone. As taught in the *Westminster Confession* (1:5-6, 10), "our full persuasion and assurance of the infallible truth and divine authority" that the Bible alone is the Word of God, "is from the inward work of the Holy Spirit bearing witness by and with the Word in our hearts" (*1 Corinthians* 2:9-10; *1 Thessalonians* 1:5; *1 John* 2:20, 27; see *Isaiah* 59:21). Then too, "we acknowledge the inward illumination of the Spirit of God to be necessary for the saving understanding of such things as are revealed in the Word" (*John* 6:45; *1 Corinthians* 2:12-15; *Ephesians* 1:18; see *2 Corinthians* 4:6). And "the supreme judge by which all controversies of religion are to be determined, and all decrees of councils, opinions of ancient writers, doctrines of men, and private spirits, are to be examined, and in Whose sentence we are to rest, can be no other but the Holy Spirit speaking in the Scripture" (*Matthew* 22:29, 31; *Acts* 28:25; see *1 John* 4:1-6).

Are we really to believe that the pope and the Roman bureaucracy are more capable of interpreting the Bible for us than the Holy Spirit speaking in Scripture? To ask the question is to answer it. In fact, Scripture itself, in various places, warns us that the visible church at times may, can, and did indeed teach falsehood (see *Jeremiah* 6:13; *Isaiah* 29:10; *Acts* 20:29; *1 Timothy* 4:1;

2 Peter 2:2; 3:15), but the Scriptures can never err. Madrid's claim, unintentional though it may be, is blasphemous. He is certainly, however, not alone in such irreverence for the Word of God. John Henry Cardinal Newman stated: "It is antecedently unreasonable to suppose that a book [the Bible] so complex, so unsystematic, in parts so obscure, the outcome of so many minds, times, and places should be given us from above without the safeguard of some authority [the Roman Church-State Magisterium]; as if it could possibly, from the nature of the case, interpret itself."[8] This is an extraordinary and telling confession. According to Newman, the Roman Church-State Magisterium is more authoritative, more capable of interpreting the Bible, than is the Holy Spirit, Who in His divine incompetence (I speak as a Romanist) has given us a "complex," "unsystematic," and "obscure" Bible that requires Newman *et alia* to explain. Apparently Newman did not consider the pontifications of the Roman Church-State complex, unsystematic, and obscure, despite being composed by so many minds, at so many different times, in so many places.

Moreover, Newman and present day Romanism ascribes a more limited authority to the Bible than did the older Roman Church-State.[9] Newman taught that although God has given us part of special revelation in the Scriptures, there is another non-propositional revelation that comes by means of "intuition." Roman Catholic theologian Hans Küng is basically of the same opinion. According to Küng, not even all the Bible is the Word of God. There is what he called the revelation, which comes by means of "the infallibility of religious encounter."

8. Cited in *Not By Scripture Alone*, 293n.
9. John W. Robbins, editor, "Beware of Men" (*The Trinity Review*, July 1999), 1.

This is, of course, Neo-orthodox nonsense. "Non-proposi-tional revelation" is a contradiction in terms. As we have shown, without propositions there can be no revelation of truth at all. Truth and knowledge come only in propositions.

Third, when we are told that "millions of ordinary Christian believers over the centuries" have found the Romish supersti-tions of transubstantiation, baptismal regeneration, the mass, the seven sacraments, the authority of the Roman Church-State, the primacy of Peter, and Sacred Tradition in the Bible, the present writer demurs. First, these are not "ordinary Christian believ-ers," because Christians do not believe such superstitions, and such superstitions are not in Scripture. This is not to say that Christians do not err in some of their beliefs; they do. But by definition, a Christian does not believe that the sacraments are necessary for salvation, that tradition has equal authority with Scripture, that the mass is a re-sacrifice of Christ, and so forth. The present writer does agree that there are persons who do believe those falsehoods. And the reason is, as Peter tells us in the only infallible Word of God, that there are those, such as the Roman Church-State, who "twist" the Scriptures "to their own destruction" (2 *Peter* 3:16).

The same applies with regard to the early church theologians. When we are told that some of these theologians found these errant doctrines in Scripture, our reply is simple: The opinions of theologians are not the standard; the Word of God alone is. One can quote early theologians contradicting themselves and each other on almost every aspect of theology. Whitaker said it this way: "Indeed, even if the fathers were opposed to us [the Protestant view, which they were not], and we could give no answer to the arguments drawn from them [which we can], this could inflict no real damage upon our cause, since our faith does not depend upon the fathers, but upon the Scriptures." We must, he went on to say, examine "all their sayings by the rule of Scripture, receiving them when they agree with it, but freely and with their good leave rejecting them whenever they exhibit marks of discrepancy."[10]

Some of the early church theologians (such as Origen[11]) also "found" the subordination of the Son to the Father, the pre-existence of souls, and universal salvation in Scripture. But that does not make these doctrines Biblical. However, as we have already seen, these theologians in general made a clear distinction between themselves and the apostles who preceded them, recognizing that the apostles were Christ's chosen vessels to give us the New Testament books.

Alleged Fallacies

Patrick Madrid continues his assault on Holy Scripture by listing a series of "Fallacies Protestants Commit in Arguing for *Sola Scriptura*," with Scripture citations to support his remarks (11-19). First, there is "'The Word of God' Fallacy." Supposedly, "the Protestant mistakenly assumes that every time the phrase 'Word of God' appears in Scripture, it refers to the Bible." However, "in reality," we are told, "most of the time, when we pay attention to the context of the passage, we see that 'the Word of God' does not refer to Scripture but to Christ, the Law, God's creative utterances, and apostolic and prophetic preaching" (11).

What shall we say to this alleged fallacy? To begin with, no Protestant that I am aware of believes that the phrase "Word of God" always refers to the Bible. Madrid has erected a straw man.

10. Whitaker, *A Disputation on Holy Scripture*, 565.
11. See E. Ferguson, "Origen," *New Dictionary of Theology*, edited by Sinclair B. Ferguson and David E. Wright (InterVarsity Press, 1988), 481-482.

Further, there is a difference between the Word of God, which is eternal (*Psalm* 119:89, 152, 160), and the Bible, which is not. The Bible is the Word of God written. If one were to destroy one paper Bible, or all paper Bibles, he would not have destroyed the eternal Word of God. One such example is given to us in Scripture in *Jeremiah* 36. The prophet was told by God to write His words in a book, and to read it to the people. Wicked king Jehoiakim, not comfortable with what had been written, had the written Word destroyed. God then told the prophet to write the Word down again. The king had destroyed the written Word, but he had not destroyed God's Word. God's Word is eternal propositions that find expression in written statements. For over 1900 years, those written statements have been only the 66 books of the Bible.

Next, we are to recognize that the eternal Word of God itself is to be worshiped (*Psalms* 56:4, 10; 119:48), because it is God Himself; it is an attribute of God (see *Psalm* 138:2). This is why Christ is called the *Logos* of God, Who is God (*John* 1:1-3). But certainly we do not worship a paper book, even the written Word of God. The Bible, as a book, is not eternal. Christians do not bow down to a book, but Romanists do.[12] Jesus Christ, the

---

12. Ironically, the Roman Church-State has made an idol of the physical Bible. The *Catholic Family Edition of the Bible*, published in 1953, and bearing the imprimatur of Francis Cardinal Spellman, Archbishop of New York, carries this introductory note: "The Holy See grants indulgences for the pious reading of the sacred Scriptures.... An indulgence of five hundred days is granted for the faithful who read at least some verses of the Gospel as spiritual reading, and in addition, while kissing the Gospel Book, devoutly say one of the following invocations.... A plenary indulgence is granted...provided they perform the above mentioned pious work each day for a month." The superstitious practice of kissing the book while mumbling a pious invocation is idolatry. It reveals the materialism of Rome.

Logos of God, however, is not the black marks on the white pages of a book. Nor is He the flickering symbols on a computer screen. Thus, it is imperative for us to distinguish between the Bible as a written document, which is the expression of the mind of God to man, and the Eternal Word of God, which is the meaning of the Bible. But we are never to separate the two, as Madrid has done. The sentences in the Bible express exactly the meaning of the Word. Scripture itself teaches us that to preach the Word is to preach Christ, and to preach Christ is to preach the Word (see *Acts* 8:4-5; 11:19-20). Christ is His Word (*John* 1:1); the Law of God is His Word (*Psalm* 1:2-3); God's creative utterances are His Word (*Genesis* 1; *Hebrews* 11:3); and the preaching of the prophets and apostles is His Word (*Jeremiah* 1:1-10; *2 Peter* 3:1-2). And how do we know all this? Only because it is written for us in the Bible. Madrid's first fallacy is itself fallacious.

Second is "The 'Bible vs. the Church' Fallacy" (12). This fallacy, we are told, "pits the Church against Scripture" (12). The reason for this is that Protestants believe the church is subordinate to Scripture, whereas Romanism thinks the Scripture is subordinate to the Roman Church-State. That is, as we noted in part one, in Roman Catholic thinking the church is prior to Scripture, wrote Scripture, and determines what is and what is not Scripture. In Reformed thought, both the Eternal Word and its expression in Scripture, the written Word, assemble the church, are received by the church, and teach us about the church.

Madrid comments that just as Scripture has its source in Christ, so also does the church; therefore [!] they are equal (thus "validating" the Magisterium of the Roman Church-State). It is true, of course, that both Scripture and the church have Christ as their source. It is also true that all creatures have Christ as their source. This does not make all creatures equal to Scripture, or one part of creation equal to another. In fact, it is only in Scripture that we learn that the church and all things have their source in Him (*Genesis* 1; *Psalm* 24:1; *1 Corinthians* 10:26). And in Scripture we are clearly told that the church is founded upon Scripture, not vice-versa (*Ephesians* 2:20). Even though it is the church (not the Roman Church-State) which has the Biblical responsibility to proclaim the Word of God (*1 Timothy* 3:14-15), there is no Biblical support for the Roman Church-State, and still less for the Roman Church's Magisterium.[13]

Third, there is "The 'All Tradition is Bad' Fallacy" (13). Protestants, we are told, disallow all tradition. When confronted with the Romanist view of the inspired Tradition, they invariably point to *Matthew* 15 and *Mark* 7, where Jesus excoriates the traditions of men, which nullify the commandments of God. Madrid would have us know that what these two Scripture passages condemn is false tradition, not tradition itself. He then cites two New Testament verses which teach us to "hold fast to the traditions" delivered by the apostles (see *1 Corinthians* 11:2; *2 Thessalonians* 2:15).

Madrid has erected a another straw man. Protestants do not maintain that "all tradition is bad." Even though no tradition of men is ever to be considered as of equal authority with Scripture, some traditions may be useful as teaching tools. As taught in the *Westminster Confession of Faith* (1:3), even the *Apocrypha* has its proper place in Reformed theology. Even though these writings, "not being of divine authority, are no part of the canon of Scripture, and therefore are of no authority in the church of

13. Romanist arguments depend on equivocal uses of the word *church* to mean, variously, "Roman Church," "congregation," "company of God's people," "apostles," etc.

God," nevertheless, they may be "made use of," just as any "other human writing." Or as stated in Article 6 of the *Belgic Confession:* "The church may read and take instruction from these [*Apocrypha*] so far as they agree with the canonical books. They are, however, far from having such power and authority that we may confirm from their testimony any point of faith or of the Christian religion."

Then, when Madrid lists *1 Corinthians* 11:2 and *2 Thessalonians* 2:15 as traditions that we are commanded to follow unhesitatingly, the present writer fully agrees. The reason for this is that they are apostolic teaching, the very Word of God, written for us in the Bible. Because they are written in Holy Scripture, and only because they are written in Holy Scripture, do we know that they are authoritative and apostolic.

Rome's attempt to elevate its vaunted "living tradition" to the level of Scripture (which by their insidious implication is dead) is not only impious, it is destructive. As Jerome taught: "All other things also, which they [the opponents of *sola Scriptura*] find or invent out of their own heads, as if it were an apostolic tradition, without the authority and testimony of Scripture, the sword of God [Scripture] strikes through."[14]

Strangely, Madrid claims that *2 Timothy* 2:2 ("And the things that you have heard from me through many witnesses, commit these to faithful men who will be able to teach others also") "not only points to the transmission of the deposit of faith through oral Tradition, it also gives us a glimpse of the beginnings of apostolic succession" (14). It does nothing of the sort. What it points to is the importance of preparing men for the eldership by teaching them a sound theology, a theology in accord with

14. Cited in Whitaker, *A Disputation on Holy Scripture*, 693.

that of Christ's apostles. And how Madrid can conclude that it "gives us a glimpse of the beginnings of apostolic succession" is stranger still. Are we to conclude that Timothy was an apostle? How about everyone that he taught? Is every teacher an apostle, along with his disciples? Not even Rome officially teaches the apostolic succession of Paul and Timothy, as Madrid does – only of Peter. Which raises the question, Why? Why are there not twelve lines of apostolic succession, rather than one? The answer, of course, is centralization of power.

Fourth, we have "The '*Sola Scriptura* is Found in the Old Testament' Fallacy" (14). Madrid asserts that "in the Old Testament God gave authority to the priests to interpret His law and issue binding doctrine based on those interpretations, even with regard to criminal and civil cases – both through divine revelation" (14). The author then adduces *Deuteronomy* 17:8-12 to prove his point. *Deuteronomy* 17 does speak to the importance of having priests present at court cases, the reason being that they were to be the teachers in Israel (*Deuteronomy* 33:10; *Malachi* 2:7); hence, they would presumably have a better grasp of the written law of God, and serve at the trial by helping the judge properly interpret the law and render just judgments. This, of course, says nothing about the infallibility of the priests, who as *Malachi* 2 teaches, often misinterpreted and misapplied the law. *Deuteronomy* 17 teaches nothing at all about infallible teachers. Rather, it instructs us as to how a Biblical court should conduct itself. Punishment should be meted out according to the judge's decision, based on Biblical law. Then when Madrid concludes from this passage, which he has wrongly interpreted, that "in the New Testament, [God] endowed the Church with a charism to teach infallibly" (14), he has abandoned logic, as well as having no New Testament support for his assertions.

The second part of this alleged Old Testament fallacy has to do with matters of divine worship. Says Madrid: "Not only are there clear references to an authoritative body of teachers (constituted by God or by His appointed prophets and kings), but there are also a number of examples in which authoritative oral Tradition is at work alongside Scripture in the Old Testament. Here are two examples: *2 Chronicles* 29:25 and *2 Chronicles* 35:4" (15). Apparently what makes these two verses "so striking" to Madrid is that God allegedly commanded reforms in worship based on oral tradition which had been preserved for centuries (back to the time of David). Yet they remained binding on the nation Israel with regard to its worship.

What is most unusual here is that Madrid does not seem to understand that when an Old Testament prophet pronounces a commandment of God, it is divine revelation, immediately given by God, not oral tradition. Because it is divine, not because it is oral, it is necessarily authoritative and binding. Divine, special revelation is now found in the 66 books of the Old and New Testaments alone. And when we read *2 Chronicles* 29 and 35 we are reading the very Word of God, which explains to us how these divinely mandated principles of worship were established. They were promulgated by God's authoritative instruments of revelation: the human (and secondary) authors of Scripture.

Furthermore, *2 Chronicles* 35:4, which Madrid cites, reads: "Prepare yourselves according to your fathers' houses, according to your divisions, following the written instruction of David king of Israel and the written instruction of Solomon his son." It requires the febrile imagination of a Romanist to transubstantiate written instructions into oral traditions. Furthermore, Madrid imagines that the "commandment of David" in *2 Chronicles* 29:25 is merely oral, but there is nothing in the text that requires that, and that interpretation is contradicted by 2 *Chronicles* 35. Ironically, Madrid appeals to the written Word to establish the alleged authority of oral tradition. Why cannot oral tradition stand on its own feet? Ethereal whispers down incensed halls are never as sure, pure, clear, permanent, or authentic as written words.

Fifth, we have "The '*Sola Scriptura* is Found in the New Testament' Fallacy" (16). "Ditto for the New Testament," claims Madrid. "After all, it's here we would expect to find the strong proof texts supporting *sola Scriptura* if, in fact, Christ and the apostles had taught and practiced it. But we don't because they didn't. There are no verses that either express or imply that Scripture is to be the sole rule of faith for the Church, especially in independence of the Magisterium and sacred Tradition." The author then goes on to claim that the book of *Acts* "describes how the Church constantly invoked apostolic authority, whether by an Apostle himself or one of his protégés (*i.e.*, the nascent Catholic Magisterium [*sic*]) in the interpretation of Old Testament Scripture" (16).

We have already seen that there are a number of New Testament texts that show that "Scripture is to be the sole rule of faith for the church." Obviously, Rome disagrees. Of course, the present writer replies, the book of *Acts* describes the invoking of apostolic authority, the reason being that the apostles are agents of revelation, themselves engaged in writing down the Word. But the apostles themselves have no magisterial authority, as one can see from *Galatians* 1. And to claim that the popes are the institutional descendants of Peter, and are therefore apostles, or are invested with apostolic authority (which amounts to the same thing) flies directly in the face of the New Testament. Why? Because according to Scripture, an apostle was one who was directly called by Christ (*Matthew* 10:1-4; *Acts* 9), and one who had personally seen the resurrected Christ (*Acts* 1:21-22; *1 Corinthians* 9:1). No pope can truthfully make such a claim. Further, in *1 Corinthians* 15:8, Paul calls himself the last apostle. That in itself should settle the matter. And when Madrid suggests that the protégés of the apostles are "the nascent Catholic Magisterium," he discloses his penchant for imaginative history.

The author cites *Acts* 15, where he maintains that at the Jerusalem council "the apostles did not invoke *sola Scriptura*. Rather, they called a plenary council to settle this doctrinal dispute." And when the final decision was made, it was not due to "thus says the Scripture," but "thus says the Holy Spirit through this council" (16-17). It is, of course, true that the matter of circumcision and its relationship to salvation was settled by the decision of a "plenary council." This is the case, even though an apostolic decision would have settled the matter just as well. One reason for holding the council is that the church is here given an example of how it should conduct itself in matters of ecclesiastical dispute through the centuries. No one leader is to make the decision, especially when lacking apostolic authority and divine revelation. And when the final decision was made, it was based on the fact that "it seemed good to the Holy Spirit, and to us" (*Acts* 15:28). But the Holy Spirit reference here is to the Holy Spirit speaking in Scripture, that is, from *Amos* 9:11-12 and *Leviticus* 17:14, found in *Acts* 15:16-17, 29. That is also why "it seemed good...to us." And that is why the decision was binding on the churches (*Acts* 16:4).

Furthermore, this decision was given in writing (verse 23) from Jerusalem (not Rome) because men had gone out from the Jerusalem church to the Gentiles orally teaching a false gospel. And this written decision was not announced by Peter, but by James, who explicitly mentioned the Old Testament as his authority.

The Biblical view of conciliar decisions is not that which is taught by Rome. Rather, it is the one taught by the *Westminster Confession of Faith* (31:1, 3-4):

> For the better government, and further edification of the church, there ought to be such assemblies as are commonly called synods and councils.
>
> It belongs to synods and councils, ministerially [not magisterially] to determine controversies of faith and cases of conscience, to set down rules and directions for the better ordering of the public worship of God, and government of His church; to receive complaints in cases of maladministration, and authoritatively to determine the same: which decrees and determinations, *if consonant with the Word of God*, are to be received with reverence and submission; not only for their agreement with the Word, but also for the power whereby they are made, as being an ordinance of God appointed thereunto in His Word.
>
> *All synods or councils, since the apostles' times, whether general or particular, may err; and many have erred. Therefore they are not to be made the rule of faith or practice; but to be used as a help in both.*

All decrees and determinations of synods and councils "if consonant with the Word of God, are to be received with reverence and submission." Since all courts, from time to time, can and do err in their decisions, no man (such as the pope) or group of men (such as a church court) may bind the conscience of a local church or church member. These decisions, therefore, "are not to be made the rule of faith and practice, but to be used as a help to both." Only God's Word is without error; it alone is to be followed with "implicit faith." Hence, all court determinations are subject to the Berean principle of *Acts* 17:11: "they searched the Scriptures daily to find out if these things [spoken by the apostles] were so."

Undaunted, Madrid continues by referring to three passages "in which the apostles prefer not to use the Scripture when teaching" (17), which he (remarkably) thinks supports the doctrine of the infallible authority of the Roman Church-State:

1 Corinthians 11:34: "And the rest I will set in order when I come."

2 John 12: "Although I have much to write to you, I do not intend to use paper and ink. Instead, I hope to visit you and to speak face to face so that your joy may be complete."

3 John 13: "I have much to write to you, but I do not wish to write with pen and ink. Instead, I hope to see you soon, when we can talk face to face."

Of course, in none of these passages do the apostles show any preference "not to use Scripture in their teaching." They express a preference, for whatever reason, not to write further to the persons addressed in these letters, but it does not follow that the later spoken teaching of the apostles was not based on Scripture – either Scripture they themselves had already written, or on the Old Testament.

What also needs to be recognized in these three passages is that in each case the one speaking is an apostle, one of Christ's ministers and an agent of special revelation. Since A.D. 100, there have been no apostles. Apostolic teaching is now found only in the writings of the apostles, which we have only in the New Testament. These teachings cannot be augmented, modified, amended, or discounted by any subsequent officers of any church or church council. These verses, therefore, affirm nothing in favor of any alleged magisterial authority in the church, for the Bible denies that there is any.

Sixth, and finally, we have "The 'Scripture Interprets Itself' Fallacy" (17). "This fallacy," writes Madrid, "is a fundamental element of *sola Scriptura*" (17). Madrid takes dead aim against the teaching of the *Westminster Confession* (1:7). If "all things in Scripture...which are necessary to be known, believed, and observed, for salvation, are so clearly propounded, and opened in some place of Scripture or other, that not only the learned, but the unlearned, in a due use of the ordinary means, may attain unto a sufficient understanding of them," how are Protestants able to explain the "vast differences that have fractured Protestantism from the start?.... By using Scripture alone, no one can know for sure which of all the many competing, squabbling Protestant sects is the right one" (18).

First, Madrid's conclusion simply does not follow from his premises. His conclusion is merely an assertion, unsupported by any valid argumentation.

Further, to read Madrid here, one would think that the Roman Church-State has always been in perfect agreement. Most emphatically, that has not been and is not now the case. Popes have disagreed with popes, to the point where at the time of the "papal schism" (1378-1409) there were three rival popes who excommunicated and anathematized each other;[15] some church traditions have been countermanded by other church traditions; councils have contradicted councils and popes; theologians have contradicted each other, order has contradicted order, and so on, *ad infinitum.*

15. Schaff, *The Creeds of Christendom*, I:181-182.

But let us concede for the sake of argument that there have been "vast differences which have fractured Protestantism." Why is this? The principal reason is that many of those who profess to be Protestants have in fact, like Madrid and Rome, rejected *sola Scriptura*, adding to and subtracting from Scripture. That is, they have adopted the Romish view that Scripture is insufficient, complicated, and obscure, and must be supplemented or corrected by extra-Biblical teaching and writing. This sinful human disposition to distort and pervert the Word of God is the reason there are so many warnings in Scripture against false teachers: *Matthew* 7:15-20; *Acts* 20:28-31; *1 Thessalonians* 5:20-21; *2 Thessalonians* 2:1-12; *2 Peter* 3:16; *1 John* 4:1-6; *2 John* 10; and *Revelation* 22:18-19, just to list a few.

Notice the diabolical shrewdness of Rome's policy: Rome has encouraged all men to think that Scripture is incomplete, insufficient, complicated, and obscure, in need of supplementation, clarification, and correction. Many believe this teaching of Rome, and proceed to supplement, "clarify" and "correct" Scripture by the opinions of scientists, archaeologists, historians, psychologists, and philosophers. Rome then blames the resulting cacophony of theologies on *sola Scriptura* and Protestantism, and argues that only Rome can bring order out of this chaos and anarchy! Like all tyrants, Rome has encouraged disorder in order to take advantage of it and consolidate its power.

To further support his claim that Scripture as its own infallible interpreter is unbiblical, Madrid cites *2 Peter* 1:20-2:1: "First of all you must understand this, that no prophecy of Scripture is a matter of one's own interpretation, because no prophecy ever came by the impulse of man, but men moved by the Holy Spirit spoke from God. But false prophets also arose among the people, just as there will be false teachers among you, who will secretly bring in destructive heresies, even denying the Master who bought them, bringing upon themselves swift destruction."

"This passage," says Madrid, "hardly needs commentary. You might think this warning contains sufficient evidence that 'destructive heresies' are the natural outgrowth of the 'every man for himself' approach to the Bible" (18-19). First, Madrid, like the Roman Magisterium, has misinterpreted the verses. *Second Peter* 1:20-21 do not deny the right and responsibility of every Christian to read and understand Scripture for himself. The warning is against church leaders – false teachers and false prophets – who claim to be the sole legitimate originators and interpreters of Scripture. Peter explicitly warns against the sort of Magisterium that the Roman Church-State claims. No divine prophetic utterance, says Peter, ever originated from man's will. Rather, the prophets of Scripture spoke as they were "moved by the Holy Spirit." In other words, as stated by Robert Reymond, in these verses "Peter totally excludes the human element as the ultimate originating cause of Scripture."[16] This is a strong warning against destructive heresies brought in by false teachers, who claim to have a unique ("private") ability to interpret Scripture – such as the priests, bishops, and popes of the Roman Magisterium.

Madrid concludes this section: "But almost as if St. Peter had foreseen the rise of Protestantism, he added another prescient warning about private interpretation" (19), in *2 Peter* 3:15-17: "There are some things in [Paul]s letters hard to understand, which the ignorant and unstable twist to their destruction, as they do the other Scriptures. You therefore, beloved, knowing this beforehand, beware lest you be carried away with the error of lawless men and lose your own stability."

16. Reymond, *A New Systematic Theology of the Christian Faith*, 38.

Once again, the question is not, Are men able to twist the Scriptures? Of course they are and they do, including, especially, church leaders. But it is not believers that Peter is speaking against in these verses. It is the Scripture-twisting false teachers (such as Roman Catholic popes) that plague the church that he warns against (see *2 Peter* 2:1-3). Peter's injunction is that each man think for himself and not be led astray by "the false teachers...who will secretly bring in destructive heresies." This is precisely why all believers are enjoined to apply the Berean principle of *Acts* 17:11. All believers have not only the right, but also the responsibility to "search the Scriptures daily to find out whether" those things they are being taught in the churches are true.

Moreover, as discussed above, Peter does not say that "all things" or "most things" that Paul wrote are "hard to understand," but only "some things." Neither does Peter say that these "some things" cannot be understood. He merely states that some parts of Scripture are harder to understand than other parts. This being so, as the *Confession* (1:9) teaches, the way to come to an understanding of these passages is by diligently applying the proper rules of Biblical hermeneutics: "The infallible rule of interpretation of Scripture is the Scripture itself: and therefore, when there is a question about the true and full sense of any Scripture (which is not manifold, but one), it must be searched and known by other places that speak more clearly."

Red Herrings

After another question-begging ipsedixitism ("this is so because I said it"): "*Sola Scriptura* is not Biblical" (19-21), Madrid calls the Reformed principle of *sola Scriptura* "canon fodder" (22). The issue here has to do with the "canon" of Scripture. "There is no 'inspired table of contents' in Scripture that tells us which books belong and which books do not" (22). Without the Magisterium of the Roman Church-State, he says, there could be no infallible knowledge of which books compose the New Testament. Once again the author takes aim against the teaching of the *Westminster Confession* (1:4-5), that ultimately "our full persuasion and assurance of the infallible truth and divine authority thereof, is from the inward work of the Holy Spirit, bearing witness by and with the Word in our hearts."

What is Madrid's response to the teaching of the *Confession?* "This is pure Mormonism – the old 'I know it's inspired because I feel in my heart that it's inspired' line that Mormon missionaries use" (22-23). The fact of the matter is, that according to the Confessional view, the determination of the canon of Scripture is not a subjective enterprise at all. It is the objective testimony of the Holy Spirit to His own infallible, inerrant Word that determines the books of the canon. Apparently Madrid believes that the witness of the Holy Spirit to His own Word is insufficient, whereas the Magisterium of Rome is sufficient. Yet, the Roman Church-State itself appeals to the Holy Spirit as its guide! On this point, the difference between Romanism and Christianity is that Rome restricts the work of the Holy Spirit to one, or a few men, the hierarchy, while Christianity teaches that every believer has and is taught by the Holy Spirit, and needs no other teacher (see *1 John* 2:26-27). Again the errors of Rome are apparent.

According to Madrid, the Magisterium of Rome is endowed with Christ's teaching authority in *Matthew* 16:18-19; 18:18; and *Luke* 10:16. The same Magisterium is allegedly promised the guidance of the Holy Spirit in *John* 14:24-25 and 16:13 (23). The first passage adduced is misinterpreted to support the Romish teaching that Jesus Christ appointed Peter as the first pope, and thereby established the papacy. Peter is the "rock" upon whom the church will be built. And all of the popes, as Peter's successors, are to be considered infallible in matters of faith and morals.[17] Of course, the passage says nothing about the papacy.

The Protestant churches, on the other hand, have consistently denied this interpretation of *Matthew* 16:18-19. The passage begins with Jesus Christ saying: "I say to you that you are Peter [*petros*], and upon this rock [*petra*] I will build My church." The first thing to note is that the Greek words *petros* and *petra*, while cognate, are not the same word. The word *petros*, by which Christ named Peter, is masculine, and refers to a boulder or rock. The Greek word *petra*, which Christ uses to refer to that rock upon which He will build His church, is feminine, and it means "bedrock." The words, while similar, are obviously not the same, regardless of what Roman Catholic apologetes would have us believe. Obviously, then, Christ is not saying that He will build His church upon Peter. Had He wished to do so, He could have simply used the personal pronoun *you* as He did in the first part of His sentence ("I say to you"). By not using "you" and by using the phrase "this rock," Christ distinguishes the rock on which his church is founded from Peter.

What then is the rock upon which the church will be built? Peter's confession answers the question for us. Just prior to Christ's pronouncement that He would build His church upon this "bedrock," the Apostle Peter had confessed "You are the Christ, the Son of the living God" (verse 16). Scripture is replete with passages telling us that God Himself is the Rock or refuge of His people (*Deuteronomy* 32:4, 15, 18, 30-31; *1 Samuel* 2:2; *2 Samuel* 22:2-3, 32, 47; 23:3; *Psalms* 18:2, 31, 46; 28:1; 31:2-3; 42:9; 61:2;

17. Boettner, *Roman Catholicism*, 104-124.

62:2; 78:35; 89:26; 92:15; 94:22; 95:1; *Isaiah* 8:14; 17:10; *Matthew* 7:24; *Luke* 6:48; *Romans* 9:33; *1 Corinthians* 10:4; *1 Peter* 2:8). Who is the Rock upon which the church of Christ will be built? It is none other than Christ Himself.[18]

This is further substantiated in *1 Corinthians* 10:4, where Paul clearly calls Christ "the Rock." And in *Ephesians* 2:20-22, the apostle states that Christ is the cornerstone of the church or temple of the Lord. The cornerstone is that stone laid at the beginning of construction by which all of the other stones in both foundation and wall are to be seated and measured. It is the standard by which all else is to be built. Peter himself says that Christ is the rock: *1 Peter* 2:8. Christ, then, the Word of God incarnate, is the Rock, the standard of all else. Roman Catholicism does indeed build upon the papacy. But the Christian church is built upon the eternal Son of God and His Word. Except a church be built upon the Rock of Christ, it is no church of His.[19]

When Jesus Christ goes on to say to all the disciples in *Matthew* 16:19 (and in 18:18),[20] "I will give you the keys of the kingdom of Heaven, and whatever you bind on Earth will have been bound in Heaven, and whatever you loose on Earth, will have been loosed in Heaven," He is referring to the apostles, those whom He has chosen as His ministers to write His Word infallibly. Hence, Christ is the Rock, and His authority is vested in His Word.

18. This was the view of Augustine, *Exposition on Psalm 61*; *Sermon 26 on New Testament Lessons*; and *On the Trinity* (II.17.28). It was also the teaching of John Calvin, *Commentary* on *Matthew* 16:18; *Institutes* IV:6:6.

19. See W. Gary Crampton and Richard E. Bacon, *Built Upon the Rock* (Blue Banner Ministries, 1999), 3-4.

20. The wording in *Matthew* 16:19 and 18:18 is very similar. The main difference is that in 16:19 the pronoun "you" is singular, and in 18:18 it is plural, showing that the apostles as a group are in view, and not just Peter.

When Madrid cites *Luke* 10:16 as a verse which teaches that Christ has endowed the Roman Magisterium with His authority, he repeats an earlier mistake. The verse reads: "He who hears you [Christ's teachers] hears Me, he who rejects you rejects Me, and he who rejects Me rejects Him [the Father] who sent Me." The teaching is manifestly apparent. To reject the Word of Christ proclaimed is to reject Christ, because Christ and His Word are one. That is why He is called the Word of God (*John* 1:1). Authority here is vested, not in an infallible church, but in Christ's infallible Word.

One might ask Madrid: What if the Word is not proclaimed accurately by church leaders? The Christian answer is: If this is the case, then it is not Christ's Word, and it does not have His authority, no matter who speaks it, including a genuine apostle or an angel (*Galatians* 1:8-9). But when the Word of Christ is faithfully proclaimed, it is just that – it is Christ's Word. And to reject the Word is to reject Christ.

As to guidance from the Holy Spirit promised to the Magisterium in *John* 14:25-26 and 16:13, a similar error is committed. As studied in part one, these verses teach us that Christ promised His apostles that He would provide His Spirit to guide them in their ministry of teaching and writing His infallible Word. We may say with Reymond that in these verses Christ "pre-authenticated" the "divine origin, inspiration, and authority" of the New Testament writings.[21] Once again, it is the Word of God that is vested with the full authority of the Son of God, not the church.

Madrid's next assault on truth occurs in "an overview of the more common Protestant arguments raised in defense of *sola*

21. Reymond, *A New Systematic Theology of the Christian Faith*, 47.

Scriptura" (23). His strongest attack is concentrated on *2 Timothy* 3:16-17, as "the verse most often used" in defense of the Protestant position. In fact, claims Madrid, "this passage is a minefield of difficulties for *sola Scriptura*" (23). The verses under study, which were written by the Apostle Paul to Timothy, a minister of the Word of God, read as follows: "All Scripture is given by inspiration of God [*theopneustos*, God-breathed], and is profitable for doctrine, for reproof, for correction, for instruction in righteousness, that the man of God may be complete, thoroughly equipped for every good work." In chapter 3, Robert Sungenis goes into much more detail on this verse (and others). Hence, Madrid's and Sungenis' analyses will be examined together.

Madrid's only substantive point is simply that "there is no way to determine who is a 'man of God,' and who isn't" (24). (If that is the case, Romanism is also refuted.) Therefore, he argues, the verses cannot possibly be all that Protestants make them out to be. That is to say, Protestant teachers differ on a number of subjects, such as infant baptism, the matter of marriage and divorce, and so forth. How are we to determine which one of these teachers is really the man of God? The argument, says he, "begs the question," because each Protestant believes that he has the correct interpretation of Scripture. Obviously they cannot all be right.

The answer to Madrid's question is rather simple: All Biblically gifted pastors and teachers are men of God. Then, too, as William Hendriksen wrote, by implication, all Christians are also considered men of God: "The man of God is the believer. Every believer, viewed as belonging to God…,is here given this title."[22] But it is not the man of God who is infallible and iner-

22. William Hendriksen, *New Testament Commentary: Exposition of the Pastoral Epistles* (Baker Book House, 1979), 303.

rant, Paul writes, it is the Word of God that is. The Protestant view is not that men of God are without error, but that by Scripture alone they are "thoroughly equipped for every good work." Men of God may indeed misinterpret Scripture, misapply Scripture, or misunderstand Scripture. But that in no way alters the teaching of 2 *Timothy* 3:16-17 that Scripture and Scripture alone is all-sufficient to equip believers "for every good work."

Twisting Scripture

Robert Sungenis takes twenty-one pages attempting to refute the Protestant interpretation of 2 *Timothy* 3:16-17 (109-130). He uses word studies, contextual analysis, comparative passages, and so forth. Some of his work is impressive; some is trite. But there are flaws throughout.

According to Sungenis, a literal rendering of 2 *Timothy* 3:17 is: "In order that the man of God may be fit, having been fully equipped for every good work" (110n). He continues by "reminding" the Protestant church that Paul is not saying that it is Scripture which is "perfect" or "complete" to "accomplish the task at hand" (113). Rather, it is the man of God who is fit and fully equipped. This, of course, is not true. The passage says that Scripture is inspired and is profitable. The man of God may by Scripture be fully equipped. That is what Sungenis' own "literal" rendering says. Both David (*Psalm* 19:7) and James (*James* 1:25) assure us that Scripture is "perfect," and Paul is clearly saying that the man of God may be "fit" and "fully equipped for every good work" by means of Scripture alone, which is inspired and infallible. This is the Protestant teaching of *sola Scriptura*.

Mr. Sungenis, either knowingly or unknowingly, separates the Word of God from the other gifts that God has given the church in his explanation of a series of verses. In *Ephesians* 6:10-18, he writes, Paul considers the Word of God as only one of a number of components of the "full armor of God" (114-115). But when the apostle lists "the belt of truth [which is Scripture]," "the breast-plate of righteousness" [which is Christ's righteousness, taught in Scripture, and received by faith alone], the shield of faith ["faith" here is the objective Word of God, the Scripture, not one's sub-jective belief]," "the helmet of salvation" [revealed only in Scrip-ture], and "the sword of the Spirit, which is the Word of God" [that is, the Scripture], he has given us a list of components all of which are either Scripture itself (as pointed out in brackets), or such things as "righteousness" and "salvation" which are taught to us only in Scripture. We may properly distinguish between righteousness, salvation, and Scripture. But we must never sepa-rate them, nor suggest that knowledge of them comes from any other source, simply because it is only in Scripture that we learn what righteousness and salvation are. This is Paul's clear teaching in *Romans* 1:16-17: "For I am not ashamed of the Gospel of Christ, for it is the power of God to *salvation* for everyone who believes...for in it the *righteousness* of God is revealed from faith to faith; as it is written 'the just shall live by faith.'" Notice that salvation and righteousness are inseparably related to the Gospel, revealed only in Scripture: "It is written."

So, when Sungenis states that "one cannot presume that a sufficiently equipped man has been made that way only by Scrip-ture" (115), he is mistaken, twisting Paul's words to his own de-struction. That is precisely what the verses say. As Calvin com-mented, in *2 Timothy* 3:16-17 Paul "asserts absolutely that the Scripture is sufficient for perfection. Accordingly, he who is not satisfied with Scripture desires to be wiser than is either proper or desirable."[23]

23. Calvin, *Commentary* on *2 Timothy* 3:17.

Sungenis asserts that there are other New Testament passages in which we are taught that men of God are equipped for good works by means other than Scripture. In *2 Timothy* 2:21 we read that one's behavior in the cleansing away of bad influences prepares one "for every good work." And in *2 Corinthians* 9:8 and *2 Thessalonians* 2:16-17 it is God's grace which provides an abundance "for every good work." Again, Sungenis has erred in separating Scripture from the other gifts God gives His church, through Scripture. One whose good behavior manifests itself because of the cleansing away of sin does so in accordance with and because of Scripture, the reason being that one cannot know what sin is except for the teaching of the Word of God. As Ernest Kevan pointed out, God's law is what defines sin: "If there is sin there also must be law, for sin is the transgression of the law (*1 John* 3:4)."[24] And as stated by the *Shorter Catechism* (Q. 14): "Sin is any want [lack] of conformity unto, or transgression of the law of God." Law, from at least the time of the Ten Commandments, which God himself directly wrote, is written.

As to God's grace providing us an abundance for every good work, that grace is given to us by means of Scripture alone. Paul teaches this in *Acts* 20:32 where he refers to God's Word as "the Word of His grace." In accord with Peter's commandment to "grow by means of grace" (*2 Peter* 3:18),[25] Reformed theologians refer to the outward means by which God grants spiritual growth to the Christian as the "means of grace." And as taught by the *Shorter Catechism* (Q. 88), there are three "means of grace:" "the Word, sacraments, and prayer." The Roman Catholic rejoinder

---

24. Ernest F. Kevan, *The Moral Law* (Sovereign Grace Publishers, 1963), 88.
25. The dative *en chariti* in *2 Peter* 3:18 is instrumental.

at this point may be that if there are three means of grace then *sola Scriptura* is disproved. Not so; because only from the Scripture do we know of and understand the sacraments, how they are to be administered, and how to pray. If one's prayers are not in accordance with the teaching of Scripture, they are non-efficacious prayers, and may be idolatrous or superstitious. As taught by the *Shorter Catechism* (Q. 99), the rule which God has given us for our direction in prayer is "the whole Word of God," but especially "that form of prayer which Christ taught His disciples, commonly called the Lord's prayer [*Matthew* 6:9-15]."[26] Apart from the information given to us in Scripture, sacraments and prayer would be nothing.

Sungenis makes a similar error in his exposition of *Romans* 15:4, which reads: "For whatever things were written before were written for our learning, that we through the endurance and the comfort of the Scriptures might have hope." Says Sungenis, Paul "is not giving us a treatise on *sola Scriptura* in *Romans* 15:4. He is merely showing some of the sources one has at his discretion for the hope that he wishes to generate within himself" (123). That is, maintains Sungenis, the Scriptures might be one source of encouragement and one source of comfort, but they are not the only source.

This, however, flies square in the face of what Paul is saying in this verse. He is specifically teaching that it is by the endurance given by Scripture and the comfort provided by Scripture that we can have hope. There is no other source mentioned by the apostle because there is no other source. Any encouragement or comfort received, which is not derived from the Scripture, is false encouragement and false comfort. To believe otherwise is

26. See Crampton and Bacon, *Built Upon the Rock*, 33.

to adopt a form of Antichristianity, secular or religious, and it is writ large through the pages of *Not By Scripture Alone*.

Having completed his analysis of *2 Timothy* 3:16-17, Sungenis attempts to support his views further by evaluating three more (main) passages which are used by advocates of *sola Scriptura*: *Acts* 17:11, *1 Corinthians* 4:6, and *Mark* 7:5-13 (130-167). I will discuss these before returning to Patrick Madrid's "macro" overview of Roman Catholic teaching.

The present writer agrees with Sungenis that *Acts* 17:11 "is touted as a definitive proof text" in favor of *sola Scriptura* (130). In this verse the Apostle Paul commends the Jews in Berea because they "were more noble than those [Jews] in Thessalonica [who, as verse 5 says, had disbelieved his teaching], in that they [the Berean Jews] received the word with all readiness, and searched the Scriptures daily to find out whether these things [being taught by Paul] were so." What Luke is saying is that the written Word is the standard by which the spoken word, even of an apostle, must be judged. Peter teaches the same thing in *2 Peter* 1:16-19.

Listing *Acts* 17:2-3 and *1 Thessalonians* 2:13 as examples, Sungenis' argument is that Paul elsewhere teaches that his spoken word is itself the Word of God, and therefore is to be considered equal to Scripture. This is not true. *Acts* 17:2-3 say: "Then Paul, as his custom was, went into them, and for three Sabbaths reasoned with them from the Scriptures, explaining and demonstrating that the Christ had to suffer and rise again from the dead, and saying, 'this Jesus Whom I preach to you is the Christ.'" Paul's preaching is derivative from the Scriptures – he reasons from the Scriptures – his teaching does not originate in some oral tradition. And his preaching – all preaching – is authoritative and true only in so far as it is derived from the Scriptures, only in so far as it consists of explaining and demonstrating from the Scriptures. We learn from the New Testament that there were many men in the early years of the church claiming apostolic authority who were not Christ's apostles. Just like present day Roman Catholicism, they were "false apostles, deceitful workers, transforming themselves into apostles of Christ" (2 *Corinthians* 11:13). Therefore, even prior to the close of the canon, all oral teaching, even the oral teaching of the apostles, was to be evaluated by the hearers in light of the written Word. Now, after the revelation has been completed, we have the teachings of Christ's apostles infallibly and permanently recorded for us in the New Testament. The deposit of apostolic teaching is Scripture alone.

But more on this can and must be said. Sungenis seems to believe the absurdity that because we preach, that these spoken words are somehow equal in power and authority to Scripture. He wants to argue that if anyone ever speaks, the spoken word is as authoritative as Scripture. But the apostles themselves, in their oral teaching, were not always infallible. They were infallible when they wrote Scripture, and they were infallible when they spoke under the inspiration of the Holy Spirit. But they did not always write Scripture, and they did not always speak under the inspiration of the Holy Spirit. Therefore, the oral teaching of the apostles themselves – let alone impostors such as Roman priests and popes today – was to be tested by Scripture.

Sungenis cites *Acts* 17:2-3 to denounce *sola Scriptura*, when the passage is every bit as strong as verse 11 favoring the Protestant view. In verses 2 and 3 we read that Paul's custom was to "reason" with persons "from the Scriptures, explaining and demonstrating [from the Scriptures] that the Christ had to suffer and rise again from the dead, and saying, 'This Jesus Whom I preach to you is the Christ.'"

John MacArthur's comments here are *apropos:* "It is highly significant that the Bereans [in *Acts* 17:11] are explicitly commended for examining Scripture. They had the priority right: Scripture is the supreme rule of faith, by which everything else is to be tested. Unsure of whether they could trust the apostolic message – which, by the way, was as inspired and infallible and true as Scripture itself – the Bereans erased all their doubts by double-checking the message against Scripture." MacArthur concludes by pointing out that "yet Roman Catholics are forbidden by their church to take such an approach."[27]

In *1 Corinthians* 4:6 Paul writes: "Now these things, brethren, I have figuratively transferred to myself and Apollos for your sakes, that you may learn in us not to think beyond what is written, that none of you may be puffed up on behalf of one against the other." After devoting 23 pages to a study of this verse, Sungenis concludes that "if *sola Scriptura* was in Paul's mind, he certainly did not make it clear to his readers." Further, he says, there are numerous translation variables for the verse; there are grammatical difficulties surrounding the verse; and there is also the problem of textual variants. Moreover, the phrase "not beyond what is written" is not found anywhere else in the New Testament. Therefore, it "is certainly ironic" that Protestants would appeal to this verse in support of their view (161-162).

First, as to translation difficulties, grammatical difficulties, and textual variants, there is no difficulty if one accepts the Majority Text, rather than the critical text, which relies heavily on a defective manuscript preserved by the Vatican. These difficulties arise only if we accept Romanist textual criticism. Second, it is

27. MacArthur, in *Sola Scriptura! The Protestant Position on the Bible*, 178.

true that the phrase "not beyond what is written"[28] is not found in any other place in the New Testament. But the phrase "it is written" (or something very similar) is found scores of times. And, as Charles Hodge commented, when this phrase is used it always refers to the written Word of God. We are then to assume that Paul is pointing his readers to the Scriptures as the sole source of "divine authority."[29]

The church at Corinth had a number of problems. One of them was the proclivity of the members to claim that they were disciples of "Paul," or "Apollos," or "Cephas," or "Christ" (*1 Corinthians* 1:12). Sadly, it was a church divided. Paul strongly warns the members against such schismatic thinking, which tended to elevate one teacher and his oral teaching against another. As Calvin said, Paul wants them to learn "that no one [should] be puffed up for his own teacher against another." Therefore, the apostle points them to the Word of God written as the only standard by which all things are to be judged. That is, they are "not to think beyond what is written."[30] Paul's com-

---

28. The Majority Text would support the translation: "not to think beyond what is written."

29. Charles Hodge, *A Commentary on 1 and 2 Corinthians* (The Banner of Truth Trust, 1988), 70.

30. Calvin, *Commentary* on *1 Corinthians* 4:6. It is most strange to read Sungenis' statement that "Ironically, John Calvin's interpretation of *1 Corinthians* 4:6 is similar to ours [Rome's]. A staunch supporter of *sola Scriptura* on theological grounds, Calvin did not see *1 Corinthians* 4:6 as supporting his argument. He said of the verse: 'The phrase, "beyond what is written," can be explained in two ways, as referring either to what Paul has written, or to the Scriptural proofs he has adduced. But because this is not very important, readers are free to choose which ever they prefer'" (161n). Sungenis misunderstands Calvin. Calvin's comment that "this is not very important" has to do with which choice the readers make: Whether it is the Scripture Paul has written or the Scripture he has adduced. In either case, it is Scripture alone

mand is issued precisely to end the factionalism and schism that characterizes the Roman Church-State and the Bishops of Rome before the emergence of the Church-State – the factionalism that says "I am of Peter" and appeals to its own extra-Scriptural statements and traditions.

Commenting on *Mark* 7:5-13,[31] Sungenis writes: "Because Jesus puts the tradition of the elders and Pharisees in a bad light, Protestants make the conclusion that Jesus casts a suspicious eye on all tradition. Despite the fact that many Protestants adhere to various traditions and confessions in their own denominations, nevertheless, when it comes to [Roman] Catholic traditions very little, if any, allowance is made" (163). The first part of this statement is simply not true. In fact, as Sungenis says, Protestants do adhere to certain confessions. Part one of this book is a commentary on what Presbyterians and some other Reformed groups consider the finest confession ever penned: the *Westminster Confession of Faith*. What Protestants deny, and what Romanists assert, is that tradition is a legitimate divine authority independent of, equal to, or superior to, Scripture. All confessions are to be considered as only subordinate standards, the Bible alone being the sole criterion of truth. This is precisely why Protestants rightly claim that "when it comes to [Roman] Catholic traditions very little, if any, allowance is made." Roman tradition claims to be the criterion, not Scripture.

And when the author later states that "despite Protestant aversion to [Roman] Catholic tradition, it remains an incontrovert-

---

which is the only standard by which all is to be judged. This is *sola Scriptura* through and through.

31. Appendix 2 of *Not By Scripture Alone*, authored by Mitchell Pacwa, also studies *Mark* 7:1-23, as well as *Matthew* 15:1-20.

ible fact that the New Testament values oral tradition and commands the church to preserve it (*2 Thessalonians* 2:15)" (165), he has made the same error we have discussed before. That is to say, Sungenis fails to recognize that the traditions spoken of in the New Testament are the authoritative teaching of Christ's apostles, His only vessels for giving us divine revelation. This tradition is preserved wholly in writing, in the New Testament alone.

In *Mark* 7:5-13, Christ attacked the Pharisees for undermining God's law by their own traditions. The Pharisees were elevating the authority of their religious fathers to that of (or above) Scripture, just as Roman Catholicism does. As the Roman Catholic Mark Shea writes: "Sacred Scripture is the written portion, but not the totality, of revelation which is given to us by the apostles with the authority of Christ Jesus Himself." (Substitute "Moses" for "Jesus Christ" and "prophets" for "apostles," and the Pharisees could not have said it better. According to Shea, the unwritten "sacred tradition" of Rome is also God's Word (169). According to Rome: "Sacred tradition and sacred Scripture form one sacred deposit of the Word of God" (208). *Mark* 7:5-13 implicitly condemn the Roman Church-State and its pharisaical view of church tradition.

Returning to Patrick Madrid's chapter in which he calls *sola Scriptura* "A Blueprint for Anarchy," he concludes his section by declaring that "sola Scriptura is unworkable." This is where "the 'rubber' of *sola Scriptura* meets the 'road' of everyday life." Can the Protestant church "show where in history *sola Scriptura* has worked?" (26).

This is a remarkable statement, one that easily could have been written by pragmatists William James (1842-1910) or John Dewey (1859-1952). As Gordon Clark taught, according to Pragmatism, "a theory is true in proportion to its success." But since such a determination is always subjective (how do we determine what "works," what is "successful," and what does not?), "what is true to one person may be false, or at least not quite so true to another."[32] The criterion is subjective.

The reply of the *Westminster Confession of Faith* (1:6) to Madrid is that when *sola Scriptura* is understood and applied, it always works. The reason is that "the whole counsel of God concerning all things necessary for His own glory, man's salvation, faith and life, is either expressly set down in Scripture, or by good and necessary consequence may be deduced from Scripture: unto which nothing at any time is to be added, whether by new revelations of the Spirit, or traditions of men." Further, states the *Confession* (1:10), *sola Scriptura* cannot possibly fail because "the supreme judge" by which all matters "are to be determined…can be no other than the Holy Spirit speaking in the Scripture." As we read in Scripture: "So shall My word be that goes forth from My mouth; it shall not return to Me void, but it shall accomplish what I please, and it shall prosper in the thing for which I sent it" (*Isaiah* 55:11).

The Foolishness of Philosophers

In chapter 2 of *Not By Scripture Alone*, Philip Blosser studies the supposed "Philosophical and Practical Problems with Sola Scriptura." He begins by giving us a brief historical background of the debate between Protestantism and Romanism. In this section he refers to the time of the Reformation as the "Great Divorce," maintaining that "the issues over which [Roman] Catholics and Protestants divided were not black and white" (31-32). This is deliberate obfuscation. The issues were jet black and

32. Clark, *Thales to Dewey*, 390.

pure white. The clarion call of the Protestant churches was *sola Scriptura* ("Scripture alone"), *sola gratia* ("grace alone"), and *sola fide* ("faith alone"), declaring them to be matters of eternal consequence. Protestantism embraced all three; Rome rejected all three. The Council of Trent spelled the Romanist position out in black and white, and repeatedly condemned Christianity. Nevertheless, Blosser commends the "fraternal [*sic*] efforts" now taking place between (alleged) Protestants, such as Charles Colson, and Roman Catholics, such as Richard Neuhaus, for attempting to work out the difficulties that exist between the two camps.

The author then goes on to lament the fact that in their stance on *sola Scriptura* Protestants have severed themselves from the "living traditions of the church" (36-42). He then comes to the main body of the chapter, where he attempts a detailed analysis of some of the philosophical and practical problems allegedly engendered by *sola Scriptura* (42-108). In conclusion, Blosser writes:

> Sola Scriptura is a philosophically incoherent and practically disastrous tradition of men. It is intellectually untenable, unbiblical, unhistorical, and the mother of ecclesiastical chaos. It has cut Protestantism off from its moorings in historic Christianity, and left it reeling in the capricious and devastating winds of doctrine that have swept across the last five centuries. It is one of the tragedies of the Reformation, not one of its necessities. By contrast, all good and true and necessary things of the Protestant experience – above all, the clarion call to personal conversion to Jesus Christ – can be preserved and exercised to full effect only by being re-established firmly upon the foundation that Christ laid for the ongoing instruction and life of His people, and that is the authority He delegated and continues to entrust to our Homeland's Embassy on earth:

> the Rock of St. Peter and the apostles united with him,
> and their delegated successors, the Pope and bishops united
> with him in the [Roman] Catholic Church (108).

Having read this paragraph, one wonders how much the on-going "fraternal efforts" are going to affect the theological stance of Blosser and the Roman Church-State. Rome has no intention of changing its views in matters such as these. One recent event supports this conclusion. *The Washington Post* reported that on October 31, 1999, four hundred eighty-two years after Martin Luther nailed his 95 theses to the chapel door of Wittenberg castle, in protest of the practices of the Roman Church-State, the leaders of the mainline Lutheran churches have declared that what Luther thought was so central to Christianity is really not serious enough an issue to divide it from Roman Catholicism. Hence, "the leaders of the modern Lutheran and Roman Catholic churches signed a document that officially settles the central argument about the nature of faith that Luther provoked. The agreement declares, in effect, that it was all a misunderstanding."[33] Very clearly it is the Lutherans, not the Roman Catholics, who have rejected their heritage.

There is, of course, no such thing as neutrality between two such disparate theologies. Christ said it this way: "He who is not with Me is against Me, and he who does not gather with Me scatters" (*Luke* 11:23). And those nominal Protestants who are fawning over the "Evangelicals and Catholics Together" movement are selling their evangelical birthright for a bowl of heretical stew.[34]

33. *The Washington Post* (November 1, 1999), A-1, 24. To its credit, the Missouri Synod Lutheran Church rejected this accord.

34. See Charles Colson and Richard J. Neuhaus, *Evangelicals and Catholics Together: Towards a Common Mission* (Word Publishers, 1996).

Let us examine Blosser's bluster. First, when he says that *sola Scriptura* is "philosophically incoherent," he means that (1) it is unbiblical and (2) logically inconsistent (43). Why is it unbiblical? Because the Bible does not teach it or assume it. Rather, the Bible "assumes a larger context of delegated authority," and the necessity of "extra-Biblical traditions" (43-49). We have already seen that the Bible does teach *sola Scriptura*, and it teaches it consistently. Further, the Bible does not in any sense assume the magisterial teaching authority of any institution, or mere man. Scripture most certainly does teach that there are God-ordained institutions: the family, the church, and the civil magistrate, to name three. But each of these Biblical institutions is governed by and is subject to the written Word of God. None of them has any authority other than the ministerial authority given it by Scripture. Neither does Scripture assume that there is any authority vested in extra-Biblical traditions. The only tradition that has binding force is that of Christ's apostles, which is now wholly inscripturated for us in the Bible. Apostolic teaching is found in the writings of the apostles, not the "living (that is, changing) voice" of Roman Catholic tradition. That tradition is riddled with contradictions and therefore false.

Why is *sola Scriptura* logically inconsistent? Because, we are told, it is both "self-referentially inconsistent," and it "involves a tacit violation of the principle of sufficient reason" (49). According to Blosser, *sola Scriptura* is self-contradictory because the Scripture does not teach it. To repeat, the Bible pervasively teaches *sola Scriptura*. Hence, there is nothing "self-referentially inconsistent" in *sola Scriptura* at all.

Then, too, we are told, Protestants claim that the Bible is the ultimate authority, but in fact they subordinate it to extra-Biblical traditions of individuals and denominations, which leads to "hermeneutical subjectivism" (50-51). The present author does not deny that all too often Protestants do subordinate the authority of the Bible to extra-Biblical traditions, leading to a form of hermeneutical subjectivism. But this is obviously done in violation of *sola Scriptura*, and in imitation of Rome, and it certainly does not and cannot undermine the principle of *sola Scriptura* itself. What sort of argument is it that attempts to refute a principle by citing the confusion of those who do not believe or practice the principle? As we have seen, the great Reformed creeds, such as the *Westminster Confession of Faith*, teach, in accord with the Bible, that the traditions of men are never to be put on a par with Scripture, and that the Bible is its own infallible interpreter.

Why does Scripture violate the principle of "sufficient reason"? Because "the Bible contains no inspired index of its own contents and cannot even be identified as a divine revelation except on extra-Biblical grounds of tradition...in violation of the *sola Scriptura* principle" (51). Along this same line of thought, *sola Scriptura* also "violates the principle of causality: that an effect can be greater than its cause. The [Roman] Church (the apostles) wrote Scripture; and the successors of the apostles, *i.e.*, the bishops of the Church, decided on the canon, the list of books to be declared Scriptural and infallible. If Scripture is infallible, then its cause, the Church, must also be infallible" (60).

This is a ludicrous argument, which only a philosopher could put forth. To claim that the Bible "cannot be identified as a divine revelation except on extra-Biblical grounds of tradition" is asinine. The Bible *explicitly identifies itself* as divine revelation hundreds of times. Does Blosser suppose that his or Rome's imaginary power to add or detract from the self-identification of Scripture matters one whit?

It is true that Scripture does not contain any inspired table of contents telling us that there are 66 books in the canon. But it is not true that the canon was decided on the grounds of extra-Biblical tradition. Rather, just as the Holy Spirit infallibly and inerrantly authored Scripture (*2 Peter* 1:20-21), He also infallibly and inerrantly preserved it for the church. The books themselves are the content of the canon. This is why the Bible itself teaches that God's Word will be preserved: "The Word of our God stands firm forever" (*Isaiah* 40:8; see also *1 Peter* 1:25; *Matthew* 5:18; 24:35). As taught in the *Confession* (1:5), "our full persuasion and assurance of the infallible truth and divine authority thereof, is from the inward work of the Holy Spirit bearing witness by and with the Word in our hearts" (see *John* 16:13; *1 John* 2:20, 27; *1 Corinthians* 2:10). Christians then, do not depend upon the church to determine what is and what is not Scripture, they depend on the author of Scripture Himself: the Holy Spirit. The argument that there is no inspired table of contents is puerile. In an ordinary book, the table of contents is compiled after the book is written, and it is presented for the convenience of the reader; it does not determine the contents of the book. *The book determines the table of contents; the table of contents does not determine the book.* The 66 books of Scripture are the contents of Scripture; they are the canon; and if one wants a table of contents for his own convenience, he may list the books himself. *The table of contents is derivative, not original; it is informative, not determinative. The books themselves are original, and they do not depend upon any table of contents.*

Blosser is also incorrect when he states that an effect cannot be greater than its cause. Science suggests that tiny microbes cause pandemics and tens of millions of deaths, changing the course of world history. And at least one king would have kept his kingdom if he had had a horse. Are not these effects greater than their causes? The whole notion of "sufficient reason" as Blosser uses it depends on the vague and undefined terms "greater" and "sufficient." It is useless in both philosophy and theology.

Blosser is also wrong when he contends that the church caused Scripture and that the bishops of the church decided on the canon of Scripture. He anachronistically refers to the apostles as the Roman Church-State. Christ's chosen apostles wrote Scripture, not the church, and certainly not the Roman Church, which did not yet exist. In fact, the church in the city of Rome was the *recipient* of Scripture written by the apostles; it was not the author of Scripture. The Apostle Paul wrote a long letter explaining justification by faith alone to the church at Rome. And as we have already seen, an apostle was one who had been directly called by Christ (*Matthew* 10:1-4; *Acts* 9), and had personally seen the resurrected Christ (*Acts* 1:21-22; *1 Corinthians* 9:1); and since Paul teaches us that he was the last of Christ's apostles (*1 Corinthians* 15:8), there can be no successors to the apostles who wrote Scripture. Thus, Blosser's premise is wrong, his history is false, and his conclusion is a lie. The church did not cause Scripture, and the church is not infallible. In fact, as the Apostle Paul maintains, the opposite is the case – the church is founded upon the teachings of Scripture (*Ephesians* 2:20). The logical inconsistency here belongs to Rome, not Protestantism.

Hence, *sola Scriptura* is not at all "intellectually untenable." There is nothing illogical about it. Neither does it beg the question, involving itself in a circular argument, as Blosser suggests (55-60). The *Westminster Confession of Faith*, for example, does not argue that the Bible is inspired because the Bible claims to be inspired as a means of proving or demonstrating its position. That would be circular argumentation. What is being said is that "the Bible and the Bible alone is the Word of God" is the axiom of Biblical Christianity. One cannot prove axioms. Blosser has obviously failed to read or understand *God's Hammer*.[35]

Second, when Blosser calls *sola Scriptura* a "practically disastrous tradition of men," he has asserted the opposite of what Scripture teaches. In point of fact, *sola Scriptura* denounces the traditions of men.

Blosser also states that the Protestant view is "unhistorical," and that it is "the mother of ecclesiastical chaos." It has left the church "reeling in the capricious and devastating winds of doctrine that have swept across the last five centuries." As far as historicity is concerned, there may indeed be good reason to assert that some of the early church theologians, even though they held to the infallibility and inerrancy of Scripture, did not embrace *sola Scriptura* as clearly as they should have. They may have given too much emphasis to tradition, even though their concept of church tradition did not elevate it to the level of infallibility (as does Roman Catholicism). But neither is there serious question that these theologians distinguished between Christ's agents of divine revelation, through whom we have the sacred canon, and later writers who have given us tradition.[36]

Too, it is unquestionably true that there is no monolithic stance within the nominally Protestant churches. There are Presbyterians, Lutherans, and Baptists. Each of these groups believes that its interpretation of Scripture is correct on the subjects that divide them. But all these groups, if they are genuinely Biblical groups, turn to Scripture as their one and only source of truth.

35. Gordon H. Clark, *God's Hammer: The Bible and Its Critics* (The Trinity Foundation, 1987).

36. See Harold Lindsell, *The Battle for the Bible*, 41-54, and Whitaker, *A Disputation on Holy Scripture*, 669-704.

Has *sola Scriptura*, then, caused this "ecclesiastical chaos"? The answer, of course, is no. The abandonment of *sola Scriptura* has caused many divisions. Incorrect interpretations of Scripture have also brought about divisions. To be sure, this is sad. But the alternative would be even sadder – that is, to bow one's knee, to commit intellectual and spiritual suicide, as Blosser has done, and to acquiesce in the superstitions and inanities of the Roman Church-State. Where have the teachings of Rome led? They have led to a denial of the Biblical teachings of *sola Scriptura, sola gratia,* and *sola fide.* They have led to a denial of the Gospel of Jesus Christ, to the idolatry of Mary and the dead, to the Inquisition, to fascism. The so-called "ecclesiastical chaos" which has arisen is not due to the principle of *sola Scriptura,* but it can occur only because of religious freedom, which Rome detests. Tyrants always regard freedom as anarchy, and Rome is a tyrant. Her sycophantic children long for the days of dungeons and dragons, when peasants knew their place, and priest were kings.

A Little Church History

To be certain, the study of extra-Biblical history is interesting and may be worthwhile, but it does not give us knowledge.[37] Nor can history ever tell us what should be the case. That is to say, what "ought to be" can never be derived from "what is." But since the Romanists want to look at history, let us spend several paragraphs discussing it, in an *ad hominem* fashion, from a different perspective. Two can play this game.

Martin Luther, in his *To the Christian Nobility of the German Nation* and *The Babylonian Captivity of the Church,* spoke about

37. See Gordon H. Clark, *Historiography: Secular and Religious* (The Trinity Foundation [1971] 1994).

three tyrannical abuses, which he called "three walls," which Roman Catholicism had erected to protect itself against all criticism.[38] These walls had not been formulated in the earliest years of Christendom, but centuries later with the coming of the papacy. First there was the distinction between the clergy and the laity; second was the sole authority of the Roman Church-State to interpret Scripture; and third was the claim that no council could be called except by a pope, and that the Church of Rome was not answerable to any council other than one called by a pope. Or to put it another way, the laity of the Roman Church-State were forbidden to read and interpret Scripture for themselves, because only the Magisterium of Rome can infallibly interpret Scripture. And the fact that only a council called by the Roman pontiff was binding meant that the clergy never would be answerable to the laymen.

Luther went on to criticize the whimsical and haphazard ways in which the Church of Rome interpreted Scripture, simply to promote its own Antichristian agenda. There was little or no concern for what Scripture actually taught.

Henry Hudson was in complete agreement with Luther when he wrote "the first five centuries of Christianity knew little or nothing about an actual supreme rulership of the Roman pope over all churches."[39] A bishop of Rome, Gregory the Great (590-604), claimed that the title "Universal Bishop" was "blasphemous, Antichristian, and diabolical by whomever assumed."[40] The history of the early church does not in any way support the idea of a supreme bishop. This was a later development, which

38. See G. A. Chan, "The New Babylonian Captivity of the Church," *The Trinity Review*, October and November 1997.

39. Henry T. Hudson, *Papal Power* (Evangelical Press, 1981), 16.

40. Hudson, *Papal Power*, 12-13.

may be traced to the infamous forgery of the Roman Church-State, the *Donation of Constantine*. The *Donation* was an eighth century fraud, wherein the Roman Emperor Constantine allegedly willed the western Roman Empire to the pope. For centuries the Roman Church-State taught that the *Donation* was genuine, and that it was the legal basis for the pope's civil authority.[41] The Roman Church-State is so arrogant and proud that it has never admitted that the *Donation* is a forgery.

Lord Acton,[42] arguably one of the greatest historians of the nineteenth century, was a member of the Roman Catholic Church all of his life. His best known aphorism is "Power tends to corrupt; absolute power corrupts absolutely." The aphorism was spoken in opposition to the papacy, and Lord Acton's criticisms of the Roman Church-State are legion. Acton, for instance, offered historical evidence to show that Pope Pius V and his adviser, Charles Borromeo, had instigated and approved murder under the guise of the Roman Inquisition. Both were later canonized as saints by the "infallible" Roman Church-State. Acton also noted that during the time of the Inquisition, some of the gravest sins were pardoned by Rome, while those who denied that the *Donation of Constantine* was genuine were sentenced to death. The *Donation* was thus put above the law of God.

Lord Acton further stated that the St. Bartholomew's Day Massacre of August 1572, in which tens of thousands of French Huguenots were massacred, was nothing less than premeditated murder in the name of Roman Catholicism. In his words, it "is the greatest crime of modern times." Moreover, history shows,

41. Hudson, *Papal Power*, 19; see also John W. Robbins, "Acton on the Papacy," *The Trinity Review* (July 1992).

42. The comments and criticisms by Lord Acton are taken from John W. Robbins, "Acton on the Papacy," *The Trinity Review* (July 1992).

said Acton, that for a period of three centuries the canon law of the Roman Church-State affirmed that the killing of a person who had been excommunicated from the Roman Church-State was not murder. In other words, legalized murder was a part of the official teaching (the sacred tradition) of Rome.

According to Lord Acton, the Vatican Council, called by Pope Pius IX in 1870, was convened for one purpose only: The pope was determined to establish himself as the infallible sovereign of the Roman Church-State. The Vatican Council was a travesty. Attempts were made by the pope to rig the council, promising titles, positions, and benefices to aid his cause. Too, the pope demanded that all debates in the council be conducted in Latin, in order to stymie and confuse the opposition.

As an historian, Acton was well aware of how sinful the popes had been, and how devastating the doctrine of papal infallibility could be. The popes had abrogated virtually every precept of morality. He concluded that "the papacy contrived murder and massacre on the largest and also on the most cruel and inhuman scale. They were not only wholesale assassins but they made the principle of assassination a law of the Christian church and a condition of salvation." Thus, Acton condemned the Vatican Council as "a conspiracy against divine truth and law." Wrote Acton: the doctrine of papal infallibility is a "soul-destroying error."

Blosser has falsely accused Protestantism of being "the mother of ecclesiastical chaos," but Robbins has correctly accused the Roman Church-State of *Ecclesiastical Megalomania*.[43] In this book Robbins reveals, in detail, the conflict that exists between Ro-

43. John W. Robbins, *Ecclesiastical Megalomania: The Economic and Political Thought of the Roman Catholic Church*. The Trinity Foundation, 1999.

man Catholic dogma and human freedom. Relying on official pronouncements of the Vatican, he demonstrates that through the centuries the philosophy of Romanism has shown itself to be hostile to constitutional government, private property, and political and economic freedom. Further, this wicked philosophy has engendered the corporate state, the welfare state, liberation theology, and fascism. In other words, human freedom cannot exist under the philosophical system of the Roman Church-State. Robbins concluded:

> The Roman Church-State is a hybrid – a monster of ecclesiastical and political power. Its political thought is totalitarian, and whenever it has had the opportunity to apply its principles, the result has been bloody repression. If, during the last 30 years, it has softened its assertions of full, supreme, and irresponsible power, and has murdered fewer people than before, such changes in behavior are not due to a change in its ideas, but to a change in its circumstances. Lord Acton noted a century ago that it was only when the Roman Church-State faced public opinion that disapproved of Church-State-sanctioned murder that it slowed its persecutions and attempted to speak with a voice less bloodthirsty. The Roman Church-State in the twentieth century, however, is an institution recovering from a mortal wound [*Revelation* 13]. If and when it regains its full power and authority, it will impose a regime more sinister than any the planet has yet seen.[44]

Another prominent historian has pointed out that the papal palace, under the virtually deified, Antichrist-like papacy, became the scene of incest, rape, and the abuse of young boys and

44. Robbins, *Ecclesiastical Megalomania*, 195.

girls.[45] It is apparent, then, that if Rome is correct and the Roman Church is to be put on a par with or above the Bible, and if the pope is infallible in matters of faith and morals, then what we have is an infallible institution engaged in murder, rape, incest, tyranny, lying, forgery, and the suppression of religious, political, and economic freedom. This is not a very pretty picture. It is certainly not a picture of a Christian institution.

One of the things that the early (post-apostolic) church anticipated was the coming of Antichrist, depicted in the writings of Daniel, Paul, and John.[46] The early church, however, produced no unified view.

As the Roman Church-State is fond of pointing out, there were a number of theological issues over which the Reformation churches divided (what Blosser calls "ecclesiastical chaos"). There were, however, several theological matters regarding which there was virtually no question. *Sola Scriptura, sola gratia,* and *sola fide* were three such doctrines. And significantly, another was the united conviction about the identity of Antichrist: The papacy of the Roman Church-State.

The reason the Reformed churches so clearly saw that the papacy was the Antichrist is that the papacy committed the soul-damning errors of denying *sola Scriptura, sola gratia,* and particularly of *sola fide.* The Lutheran theologian Francis Pieper expressed the view of the Reformation when he wrote:

> There can be no greater enemy of the church of God than the papacy. In and by the doctrine of justification [by

---

45. Ivan Cloulas, *The Borgias,* cited in Rousas John Rushdoony, *The Institutes of Biblical Law: The Intent of the Law* (Ross House Books, 1999), 132.

46. The quotations found in the following paragraphs on the Antichrist are taken from "Antichrist," *The Trinity Review,* edited by John W. Robbins (October 1994).

faith alone] the church lives.... Can anything worse befall the church than being robbed of the doctrine of justification [by faith alone], by which alone she lives and exists? When the enemy takes my earthly life, he can do me no greater harm in earthly matters. And when the pope has taken away the spiritual life of the church by robbing her of the doctrine of justification [by faith alone], the climax of harm has been reached.

An English theologian of the nineteenth century, H. Grattan Guinness, wrote:

> From the first, and throughout, that movement [the Reformation] was energized and guided by the prophetic Word [*sola Scriptura*]. Luther never felt strong and free to war against the papal apostasy till he recognized [in Scripture] the pope as Antichrist. It was then he burned the papal Bull. Knox's first sermon, the sermon which launched him on his mission as a Reformer, was on the prophecies concerning the papacy. The Reformers embodied their interpretation of prophecy in their confessions of faith [it also appeared in later confessions such as the *Westminster Confession of Faith*, *The Savoy Declaration*, and *The 1689 London Baptist Confession*], and Calvin in his *Institutes*. All the Reformers were unanimous in the matter.... And their interpretation of these prophecies determined their reforming action.
>
> It nerved them to resist the claims of that apostate church to the uttermost. It made them martyrs; it sustained them at the stake. And the views of the Reformers were shared by thousands, by hundreds of thousands. They were adopted by princes and peoples.

The study of history does not support the claims of the Roman Church-State. It surely appears that "the capricious and devastating winds of doctrine" that have wreaked havoc in the church and in the world at large have been the doctrines of Roman Catholicism, not Christianity.

Blosser concludes his denunciation of the Protestant doctrine of *sola Scriptura* with the audacious claim that "all the good and true and necessary things of the Protestant experience [*sic*] – above all, the clarion call to personal conversion to Jesus Christ – can be preserved and exercised to full effect" only if one returns to the doctrine taught by the Roman Church-State.

In response, first, Protestantism does not teach that "personal conversion to Jesus Christ" is an "experience." That is the position of Rome, which combines and confuses justification, regeneration, and sanctification. In Roman Catholic theology, when a sinner exercises his free will, and makes a decision for Christ, and when he is baptized, righteousness is infused into the recipient, actually "making" him righteous, and it is this infused righteousness that is the basis of justification. Christianity, on the other hand, maintains that regeneration is never consciously experienced, and that justification is forensic. It is an act of God completely external to man. In justification, God declares the elect sinner righteous because of the fact that Jesus Christ has merited salvation in the sinner's behalf. Sanctification, which as the *Shorter Catechism* (Q. 35) teaches, "is the work of God's free grace, whereby we are renewed in the whole man after the image of God, and are enabled more and more to die unto sin, and live unto righteousness," is distinct from justification.

Second, because of what we have just seen, if one accepts the teachings of Roman Catholicism, he will necessarily be lost. Simply stated, Rome is preaching "another gospel." And as Paul writes in *Galatians* 1:8-9: "If anyone preaches any other gospel to you than what you have received [the Gospel of justification by grace through faith alone in Jesus Christ alone], let him be accursed." The "gospel" of Rome is a false gospel, anathematized by Scripture itself. No wonder Roman Catholics have such a low view of Scripture.

Tradition

In chapter 4, Mark Shea asks, "What is the Relationship Between Scripture and Tradition?" His conclusion is that "in Scripture, as today, it is human tradition, not Sacred Tradition, that is condemned by Christ and His Church. In Scripture, as today, Sacred Tradition and Sacred Scripture form one sacred deposit of the Word of God" (208). We have already refuted this statement. We have seen that the tradition that the Bible enjoins us to keep is the apostolic tradition, which, since the close of the canon in the first century, is expressed only in the Bible. All other religious tradition is, therefore, human tradition, and as Jerome taught, must be subject to "the authority and testimony of Scripture."[47] No tradition outside of Scripture is to be put on a par with Scripture.

Chapter 5 is titled "Point/Counterpoint: Protestant Objections and Catholic Answers," authored by Robert Sungenis. The author cites 75 objections launched by Protestants, regarding Scripture, tradition, the canon, and the early church theologians (211-324). In various sections of this book we have already encountered and answered these in some detail. Nevertheless, several comments will be made. First, the present author agrees with Sungenis when he speaks of "how different are the

---

47. Cited in Whitaker, *A Disputation on Holy Scripture*, 693.

definitions of *sola Scriptura* offered by different Protestant theologians" (212). Sadly, there is confusion that exists among those
who ought to know better. Suffice it to say that when we speak
of *sola Scriptura* we mean that the Bible and the Bible alone is
the Word of God written, with all of the attributes discussed in
part one of this book. There is no knowledge to which we have
access, this side of the final state, other than Scripture. The study
of science does not give us knowledge; the study of extra-Biblical history does not give us knowledge; the study of the Koran
does not give us knowledge; the study of papal encyclicals and
conciliar documents does not give us knowledge; the study of
philosophy does not give us knowledge; and so forth. Knowledge is found in the 66 books of the Bible alone. Again, to cite
the definition of the *Westminster Confession* (1:6): "The whole
counsel of God concerning all things necessary for His own
glory, man's salvation, faith and life, is either expressly set down
in Scripture, or by good and necessary consequence may be
deduced from Scripture: unto which nothing at any time is to
be added, whether by new revelations of the Spirit, or traditions
of men." What could be more plain than this?

Second, the Bible speaks of the apostolic traditions which are
to be adhered to in various places (see *1 Corinthians* 11:2;
2 Thessalonians 2:15; 3:6). It also warns against the traditions of
religious men (*Matthew* 15:1-9; *Mark* 7:5-13). As we have discussed, there are no longer apostles (Christ's agents of divine
revelation); Paul claimed to be the last one (*1 Corinthians* 15:8).
Rome teaches that the popes are the successors of Peter; hence,
when they speak on matters of faith and morals they speak as
infallibly as did Peter and his fellow apostles. Church tradition,
then, is as authoritative as Scripture. This is a false and heretical
doctrine. The religious traditions of Rome are extra-Biblical tra-

ditions, are not to be considered equal to the Word of God, and are to be tested by the written Word of God.

Third, Rome claims that the Bible is a collection of inspired books, with the infallible Roman Church-State, not the books themselves, being the determiner of the canon. As cited in the *Catechism of the Catholic Church*, "it was by the apostolic Tradition that the Church discerned which writings are to be included in the list of the sacred books [which includes the *Apocrypha*]."[48] G. I. Williamson commented: "The Roman Catholic Church nowhere reveals its supreme audacity more clearly than it does here. Rome says that the Bible is the Word of God. But it also says that the certainty of this is dependent upon the testimony of the church."[49] Roman Catholicism would have us believe that God cannot guarantee His own writings by the writings themselves, but requires the Roman Church-State to do so.

Fourth, as we have studied the history of the early church theologians we have seen that they gave more credence to tradition than they should have. Nevertheless, they did not believe that the *Apocrypha* should be included in the canon, and neither did they consider the writings of later men to be on a par with the 66 books of the Bible. Moreover, when we study history (in an *ad hominem* fashion), it discloses the theological, ecclesiastical, social, and political atrocities committed by the Roman Church-State.

48. *Catechism of the Catholic Church*, paragraph 120.
49. Williamson, *The Westminster Confession of Faith for Study Classes*, 7.

The Reformers

Chapter 6 of the book is by Robert Fastiggi: "What Did the Protestant Reformers Teach about Sola Scriptura?" In this chapter Fastiggi seeks to show that the Reformers themselves were inconsistent with regard to this Reformed principle. He writes: "All Protestant groups emphasized the authority of Scripture, and some, quite explicitly, endorsed the principle of *sola Scriptura*. We will observe, however, that Protestants did not always follow this principle consistently and they often made implicit appeals to an authority other than Scripture" (326).

The first rejoinder of the present writer is that no sinner is perfectly consistent with his axioms. All the redeemed saints of God err in their thinking, simply because they are sinners. This is why it is imperative that we never rely upon the teachings of any church or man, as Rome contends we must do, but only upon the written Word of God. As taught in the *Westminster Confession* (31:4): "All synods or councils, since the apostles' times, whether general or particular, may err; and many have erred. Therefore they are not to be made the rule of faith or practice; but to be used as a help in both."

Second, the fact that some of the Reformers may have been inconsistent in their thinking with regard to *sola Scriptura* does not disprove the principle itself. By what convoluted argument can a man's failure to adhere to a principle consistently be used to show the falsity of the principle? Sinful persons, by way of analogy, err in their use of arithmetic. But their errors do not undermine the laws of arithmetic, which are fixed and established in the infallible, inerrant Scriptures.

Third, some of Fastiggi's examples of inconsistencies are not inconsistencies on the part of the Reformers at all. They are, in fact, inconsistencies on the part of Fastiggi. Fastiggi begins with Martin Luther, who at the Diet of Worms stated:

> Your Imperial Majesty and Your Lordships demand a simple answer. Here it is, plain and unvarnished. Unless I am convinced of error by the testimony of Scriptures or (since I put no trust in the unsupported authority of the Pope or of councils, since it is plain that they have often erred and often contradicted themselves) by manifest reasoning, I stand convicted by the Scriptures to which I have appealed, and my conscience is taken captive by God's Word. I cannot and will not recant anything, for to act against one's conscience is neither safe for us, nor open to us. On this I take my stand, I can do no other. God help me. Amen (327).

"It is important...to see," says Fastiggi, "that Luther also appeals to two other sources of authority other than Scripture: namely, 'manifest reasoning,' and 'conscience'" (327). One need only read Luther's statement to see that this is not the case. Luther's appeal is to Scripture alone. He clearly says that his "manifest reasoning" is convicted "by the Scriptures," and that his conscience "is taken captive by God's Word." Logic is not something added to the Scriptures (Fastiggi's argument here is an echo of some Baptists),[50] but the way in which God thinks, revealed in Scripture. Luther's statement is *sola Scriptura* at its finest.

The author correctly states that Martin Luther regarded the *Epistle of James* as "an epistle of straw" (328). But Luther was not denying the principle of *sola Scriptura* by making this claim. He

---

50. See "Are Baptists Rational?" in *Against the Churches: The Trinity Review, 1989-1998*. John W. Robbins, editor (The Trinity Foundation, 2002).

questioned the quality of *James*, considering it to be of lesser value than other New Testament books. And in point of fact, Luther later recanted of this opinion.[51]

Another theological "tension" that we find in Luther, so we are told, is that he used the phase "Word of God" in various ways. Sometimes he used it when referring to Christ's message of salvation, sometimes he spoke of the second Person of the Trinity, sometimes he used it with regard to power as manifested in God's creation of all things, and sometimes it meant Scripture itself (330). We have been over this before. But to repeat, all of these are the Word of God. We distinguish between Christ and His written Word, but we must never separate them because they are both the Word of God. The written Word – the *logos-rheemata* – is the expression of the *Logos*. Too, the message of salvation is obviously the Word of God. And we are taught in *Genesis* 1 that God created the universe by means of His Word (see also *Hebrews* 11:3). But it is the same Word. Further, the only reason we know that these things are true is that we are taught them in the Word of God written.

Having finished with Martin Luther, Fastiggi turns his pop-gun on John Calvin. "Without doubt," he writes, "John Calvin (1509-1564) was the most influential of the Reformed theologians" (339). And so he was. Calvin erred though, we are told, in his misunderstanding of the formulation of the canon. He militantly taught against the Roman Catholic view that "the credibility of Scripture depends on the judgment of the church." Such a notion, said Calvin, "is an insult to the Holy Spirit" (339-340).

51. See R. C. Sproul, *Essential Truths of the Christian Faith*, 23, and James Orr, *Revelation and Inspiration* (Eerdmans, 1952), 208.

The present writer, of course, agrees with Calvin on this point. Fastiggi does not. Calvin's error, says he, "sets the Church up against the Holy Spirit as if the leaders of the Church could not be guided by the divine Spirit in discerning the canon of Scripture" (340). Calvin does no such thing. He does not deny that the Holy Spirit can guide the church – all the church, not just Fastiggi's episcopally ordained leaders – to recognize the books of the canon. Calvin simply says that this did not occur as Rome teaches. It is not only the leaders of the church who are guided by the Holy Spirit; according to Scripture, every believer is guided by the Holy Spirit. As summarized in the *Confession* (1:5): "*Our full persuasion and assurance of the infallible truth and divine authority thereof, is from the inward work of the Holy Spirit bearing witness by and with the Word in our hearts.*" The Westminster Assembly's use of the pronoun *our* is telling. It is not just church leaders, but all of God's people ("our") who receive "the inward work of the Holy Spirit bearing witness by and with the Word in our hearts." Rome wants to claim a monopoly on the Holy Spirit. The Bible teaches that every believer is taught by the Holy Spirit.

Calvin also erred, says Fastiggi, in that he "does not consider that in the early Church there were disputes as to whether certain writings (e.g., *Hebrews*, *2 Peter*, and *Revelation*) belonged in the New Testament canon" (340). Again, Calvin does not err here. The issue is not whether there have been disputes over various books of the Bible or not. The issue is, as taught by the *Confession* (1:8), that God has "by His singular care and providence, kept [His Word] pure in all ages." And this Word consists of the 66 books of the Old and New Testaments. Calvin did not question any of them as being a part of the canon or suggest that other books be added to the canon. Parenthetically, it is interesting that the early church theologians (who, as we have seen, Rome enjoys selectively quoting with regard to its view of tradition), did not view the *Apocrypha* as part of the canon, while the Roman Church-State does.

Finally, says Fastiggi, when Calvin appeals to *Ephesians* 2:20, which states that the church has "been built on the foundation of the apostles and prophets, Jesus Christ Himself being the chief cornerstone," to support his view of the formulation of the canon, he errs. This verse, we are told, "in no way precludes the authority of the Church from establishing the canon of Scripture" (341). On the contrary, Fastiggi, that is precisely what it precludes, for Paul teaches that the church is founded upon Scripture, not Scripture upon the church.

Later in this chapter Fastiggi quotes Harry Gamble, an alleged Protestant theologian writing for *The Anchor Bible Dictionary*, to show that there is confusion even in the Protestant camp in the matter of the formulation of the canon:

> The criterion of orthodoxy signified that no document could be acknowledged as authoritative unless it conformed to, or at least did not contradict, what the church took to be its proper teaching. This presumes that the true faith of the church could be known independently of Scripture specifically in what was known as "the rule of faith" (regula fidei), a traditional summary statement of the basic Christian confession. Hence there was no idea that Scripture was the sole depository of authoritative teaching. Rather, the authority of Scripture could be gauged against authoritative but unwritten tradition (346).

According to Gamble (and Fastiggi), it is now acknowledged that the bishops needed to discern whether certain writings were in conformity with what the church already knew as a "rule of faith." The leaders, then, had to turn to unwritten tradition to determine what would stand the test and become written Scripture. Hence, concludes Fastiggi, "it is clear that the *sola Scriptura* principle was not operative in the early Church" (346).

The shame of the matter is, as the perceptive reader will recognize, that Gamble has not explained the Protestant view of the formation of the canon, but the Romanist view. This is not surprising coming from *The Anchor Bible Dictionary*, which is known for its liberal/modernist bent. Further, *The Anchor Bible Dictionary* is replete with writings of Jewish and Roman Catholic authors, as well as (supposed) Protestants. So this *Dictionary* cannot be expected to give us a genuinely Protestant, Reformed, and Christian view of anything having to do with Scripture.

Fastiggi next criticizes the *Westminster Confession of Faith*. He fully concurs that "perhaps the clearest and most complete expression of the Calvinist/Reformed understanding of *sola Scriptura* is to be found in the Westminster Confession of Faith of 1648" (343-344). But he alleges that there is inconsistency found within the first chapter "Of the Holy Scripture." That is to say, the chapter itself makes "the distinction between those parts of Scripture whose meaning is clear and those parts whose meaning is not clear" (345). This is hardly an inconsistency. The *Confession* does not say that some parts of Scripture require an ecclesiastical interpreter. Rather, what it states is that some parts of Scripture are more clear than others. As stated in Section 7 in "Of the Holy Scripture," we read:

> All things in Scripture are not alike plain in themselves, nor alike clear unto all: yet those things which are necessary to be known, believed, and observed for salvation, are so clearly propounded, and opened in some place of Scripture or other, that not only the learned, but the unlearned,

in a due use of the ordinary means, may attain unto a
sufficient understanding of them.

One Section earlier the *Confession* (1:6) claimed that "the whole
counsel of God concerning all things necessary for His own
glory, man's salvation, faith and life, is either expressly set down
in Scripture, or by good and necessary consequence may be deduced from Scripture: unto which nothing at any time is to be
added, whether by new revelations of the Spirit, or traditions of
men." This being the case, it is abundantly obvious that the
Confession is not saying that to discern the meaning of some parts
of Scripture we must rely on some extra-Scriptural authority.

Moreover, in Section 9 the Westminster divines state: "The
infallible rule of interpretation of Scripture is the Scripture itself: and therefore, when there is a question about the true and
full sense of any Scripture (which is not manifold, but one), it
must be searched and known by other places that speak more
clearly." Is it not clear to the reader that the *Confession* here states
that those places that are not as clear as others may become clear
by comparing Scripture with Scripture? Fastiggi's claim is false.
Is it not also obvious that the *Confession* says what may be more
clear and less clear varies from person to person? It is not the
text, but the noetic effects of sin that make this variation.

Then too, it is important for us to realize that when the
Westminster Assembly says that "those things which are necessary to be known, believed, and observed for salvation, are so
clearly propounded, and opened in some place of Scripture or
other, that not only the learned, but the unlearned, in a due use
of ordinary means, may attain unto a sufficient understanding
of them," it is speaking of more than conversion and justification.
In a Reformed and Christian worldview, the concept of "salvation" relates to all of life. This includes election, calling, regen-

eration, and sanctification, as well as justification. It covers every aspect of life. The Puritans of the Westminster Assembly certainly believed that the Bible teaches us about the only means of redemption: The meritorious work of Jesus Christ. But the Bible is not exclusively redemptive in its teaching. It teaches us "the whole counsel of God concerning all things necessary for His own glory, man's salvation, faith and life." This is quite evident, for example, in the teaching of the *Confession* (19:6) with regard to the "Law of God": "Although true believers be not under the law, as a covenant of works [to earn or keep salvation], to be thereby justified and condemned; *yet is it of great use to them, as well as to others; in that, as a rule of life informing them of the will of God, and their duty, it directs and binds them to walk accordingly.*"

The Foolishness of Priests

In chapter 7 of *Not By Scripture Alone*, authored by Peter Stravinskas, a Roman priest, we are taught about Roman Catholicism's "Official Doctrine on Scripture and Tradition." After reviewing the Roman Catholic position which stresses "the coordination and interplay of Scripture, Tradition, and Magisterium" (387), Stravinskas reaches his "Conclusion." In it we read:

> In discussions on Scripture and Tradition, one is often reminded of the classical debate: "Which came first? The chicken or the egg?" Both can touch off endless disputations and are largely irresolvable, but to make some sense of it all, we can resort to a temporal mode to find a way through the impasse.
>
> Clearly, Tradition precedes Scripture from the point of view of time – and the Church precedes both, in that the

writing of the New Testament did not begin until some fifteen to twenty years after the Pentecostal formation of the Church and may not have been completed until perhaps as late as A.D. 120. The Gospel message, then, was imparted through oral tradition first, and only later was it committed to written form. The means (whether oral or written), however, is in many ways secondary to the goal (Revelation) and to the receiver of the Revelation (God's people, the Church).

For Christians, the Bible is not Revelation in itself; for us, Revelation is a Person, not a book – no matter how holy. To worship a book is bibliolatry. A truly accurate and truly Christian perspective on Revelation takes all these seriously: God, the Church, the Church's Tradition, and the Church's Scriptures. The focus of our attention, however, is not the Church, the Scriptures, or Tradition, but God. The other three are means given to us to arrive at our end – union with God (387-388).

In analyzing these pious paragraphs, we begin by pointing out the skepticism of Stravinskas. Apparently he believes that the question posed is "largely irresolvable," and that we need to "resort to a temporal mode to find a way through the impasse." This is simply not so; Scripture answers the questions for us. In fact, Stravinskas appeals solely to Scripture for his "temporal mode."

First, if Stravinskas held to the principle of *sola Scriptura* he would have no problem with the conundrum "Which came first – the chicken or the egg?" *Genesis 1* teaches us that the chicken came first. Next, we assure Stravinskas that with regard to the question concerning which came first, Scripture or Roman tradition, again the matter is clear. Scripture comes first, by centuries. Even the apostolic preaching and teaching, which is not to be confused with Romanist traditions, is based on the written Word – see *Acts* 17 – and the preaching of Jesus Himself – see the *Gospels* – is based on the written Word. Jesus' first sermon is from *Isaiah* (*Luke* 4:16-21); His last words are from the *Psalms* (*Matthew* 27:46). Neither did the church precede the infallible written Word of God in that the church is "built on the foundation of the apostles and prophets, Jesus Christ Himself being the chief cornerstone" (*Ephesians* 2:20).

It is deliberately misleading to say that the Gospel message "was imparted through oral tradition first, and only later was it committed to written form." The Romanists are inventing oral tradition when there is none. The Gospel was preached from the Old Testament, and a few years later the New Testament was written as an apostolic commentary on the Old Testament. The "apostolic tradition" was taught by Christ's chosen instruments to preach, teach, and write His infallible Word. And most assuredly "the means" is in no way "secondary to the goal (Revelation) and to the receiver of the Revelation (God's people, the Church)." As Paul teaches in *2 Timothy* 3:16: "All Scripture [revelation] is given by inspiration of God [the means]." And as Peter claims in *2 Peter* 1:21: "For prophecy [revelation] never came by the will of man, but holy men of God spoke as they were moved by the Holy Spirit [the means]." According to the apostles of Christ, the means by which revelation is given is crucial to the understanding of what Scripture is. If it is not a "God-breathed (or inspired)" revelation, a revelation where the human authors are "moved by the Holy Spirit," then according to the principle of *sola Scriptura*, it is false; it is not a revelation of the triune God of Scripture at all.

The final paragraph is perhaps the most telling of all. The shadow of Karl Barth[52] (and Neo-orthodoxy) looms large over these final sentences. As we have seen, in the Neo-orthodox view, the Bible is itself not the Word of God. Parts of the Bible may subjectively "become" the Word of God (different parts for different hearers at different times), but we cannot say that the Bible is the Word of God in any objective sense. Truth is personal, not propositional. According to Neo-orthodoxy, Jesus Christ, the Word of God incarnate, is the only true revelation of God to man. And when Scripture "reveals" Christ to the reader ("the Christ event"), then the Bible becomes the Word of God to him (in a subjective sense). Therefore, when we read Stravinskas' statement that "Revelation is a Person, not a book," we fear that on top of all of the other superstitions and heresies that possess Rome, Neo-orthodoxy is one of the legion.

It is not possible for us to know who Jesus Christ is without the written Word of God. Neither is it possible to come to a saving knowledge of God without the written Word. As Paul proclaimed: "I am not ashamed of the Gospel of Christ, for it is the power of God to salvation for everyone who believes, for the Jew first and also for the Greek. For in it [the Gospel] the righteousness of God is revealed from faith to faith" (*Romans* 1:16-17). One does not come to a saving knowledge of Jesus Christ by believing in a Person without believing in the propositions which teach us about Christ in the written Word of God. The Scriptures, Paul wrote, "are able to make you wise for salvation through faith which is in Christ Jesus" (*2 Timothy* 3:15). Believing Christ

52. See Gordon H. Clark, *Karl Barth's Theological Method* (The Trinity Foundation [1963] 1997).

is believing these Scriptural propositions, and believing these Scriptural propositions is believing Christ.[53]

Further, Stravinskas is correct when he avers that "to worship a book is bibliolatry." Biblical Protestants, however, do not worship a book. To be sure, they worship the Word of God (*Psalms* 56:4, 10; 119:48), which is eternal and God Himself. But the Bible itself, as a physical book, is not eternal. To be certain, it is the Word of God written. But if one were to destroy a Bible, he would not have destroyed the Word of God. God and His Word are eternal and cannot be destroyed. Yet the Roman Church-State inculcates idolatry by offering plenary indulgences for kissing a physical book while mumbling a prayer.

Finally, when the author writes that "the focus of our attention, however, is not the Church, the Scriptures or Tradition, but God. The other three are means given to us to arrive at our end – union with God," again he errs. As we discussed in part one, epistemology (the theory of knowledge) must always come first. Without the sound epistemic base of Holy Scripture and Holy Scripture alone, we cannot know what the church is or Who God is. Neither can we know what it means or if or how it is possible to have "union with God." In point of fact, if one is to follow the teachings of the Roman Church-State, then he will never have the saving union with God that Scripture speaks about, for Rome's gospel is another gospel. It is not the Gospel taught by Christ and His apostles. It is the gospel being proclaimed by latter day false apostles, those "who come to you in sheep's clothing, but inwardly they are ravenous wolves" (*Matthew* 7:15).

53. See Gordon H. Clark, *The Johannine Logos* (The Trinity Foundation [1972] 1989).

Conclusion

In our study of the Protestant doctrine of *sola Scriptura* we have seen, as taught by the *Westminster Confession of Faith*, that the Bible and the Bible alone is the Word of God. We have considered the necessity of Scripture, the identity of Scripture, the inspiration of Scripture, the authority of Scripture, the self-authentication of Scripture, the sufficiency of Scripture, the clarity of Scripture, the transmission and preservation of Scripture, the interpretation of Scripture, and the finality of Scripture. All of these attributes are essential for a proper understanding of the *sola Scriptura* view of the Word of God.

We have studied epistemology (the theory of knowledge) and seen that the apostles and the prophets taught that the Bible has a systematic monopoly on truth. Writes Paul: "All the treasures of wisdom and knowledge" are hidden in Christ, the Word of God incarnate, Who has given us the Word of God inscripturated (*Colossians* 2:3). And "all Scripture...thoroughly equips [us] for every good work" (2 *Timothy* 3:16-17). In Biblical Christianity there is no multi-source theory of knowledge. Jesus teaches: "Your [God's] Word is truth" (*John* 17:17).

We have also seen that the Roman Church-State has attacked the Christian view, demeaning or denying each and every one of the attributes of Scripture mentioned above. The fact is that Romanism and historic Christianity have different Bibles. Christianity teaches that the Bible consists of 66 books. Rome avers that the Bible consists of 73 books (and then some), and it reserves the right to add to and subtract from the Scriptures in the future.

Rome teaches that it determined and authenticated the books of the Bible, and that only the Magisterium of the Roman

Church-State can properly interpret Scripture. Christianity, on the other hand, says that all the books of the Bible are logically prior to the Christian church, most are chronologically earlier than the Christian church, and all preceded the Roman Church-State by centuries. The Christian church is founded on Scripture; that is, Scripture authenticates and judges the church, not vice-versa. Further, every individual Christian has not only the right and privilege, but also the responsibility to study and interpret the Bible for himself. It is apparent that Roman Catholicism and Christianity have nothing in common when it comes to the doctrine of Scripture.

Roman Catholicism's rejection of the Christian doctrine of *sola Scriptura* leaves its members, like the prodigal son of *Luke* 15, starving in a far country. This rejection has led to numerous false and heretical doctrines, including a denial of the sovereignty of God, and an assertion of human independence of God. The controversy over Scripture is no intramural debate. The acceptance or rejection of the principle of *sola Scriptura* is a principial difference between Christianity and all pagan religions.

SOLI DEO GLORIA

Index

Scripture Index

The Crisis of Our Time

HISTORIANS have christened the thirteenth century the Age of Faith and termed the eighteenth century the Age of Reason. The present age has been called many things: the Atomic Age, the Age of Inflation, the Age of the Tyrant, the Age of Aquarius; but it deserves one name more than the others: the Age of Irrationalism. Contemporary secular intellectuals are anti-intellectual. Contemporary philosophers are anti-philosophy. Contemporary theologians are anti-theology.

In past centuries, secular philosophers have generally believed that knowledge is possible to man. Consequently they expended a great deal of thought and effort trying to justify knowledge. In the twentieth century, however, the optimism of the secular philosophers all but disappeared. They despaired of knowledge.

Like their secular counterparts, the great theologians and doctors of the church taught that knowledge is possible to man. Yet the theologians of the present age also repudiated that belief. They too despaired of knowledge. This radical skepticism has penetrated our entire culture, from television to music to literature. *The Christian at the beginning of the twenty-first century is confronted with an overwhelming cultural consensus — sometimes stated explicitly but most often implicitly: Man does not and cannot know anything truly.*

What does this have to do with Christianity? Simply this: If man can know nothing truly, man can truly know nothing. We cannot know that the Bible is the Word of God, that Christ died for his people, or that Christ is alive today at the right hand of the Father. Unless knowledge is possible, Christianity is nonsensical, for it claims to be knowledge. What is at stake at the beginning of the twenty-first century is not simply a single doctrine, such as the virgin birth, or the existence of Hell, as important as those doctrines may be, but the whole of Christianity itself. If knowledge is not possible to man, it is worse than silly to argue points of doctrine – it is insane.

The irrationalism of the present age is so thoroughgoing and pervasive that even the Remnant – the segment of the professing church that remains faithful – has accepted much of it, frequently without even being aware of what it is accepting. In some religious circles this irrationalism has become synonymous with piety and humility, and those who oppose it are denounced as rationalists, as though to be logical were a sin. Our contemporary anti-theologians make a contradiction and call it a Mystery. The faithful ask for truth and are given Paradox and Antinomy. If any balk at swallowing the absurdities of the anti-theologians who teach in the seminaries or have graduated from the seminaries, they are frequently marked as heretics or schismatics who seek to act independently of God.

There is no greater threat facing the church of Christ at this moment than the irrationalism that now controls our entire culture. Totalitarianism, guilty of tens of millions of murders – including those of millions of Christians – is to be feared, but not nearly so much as the idea that we do not and cannot know the literal truth. Hedonism, the popular philosophy of America, is not to be feared so much as the belief that logic – that "mere human logic," to use the religious irrationalists' own phrase – is futile. The attacks on truth, on knowledge, on propositional revelation, on the intellect, on words, and on logic are renewed daily. But note well: The misologists – the haters of logic – use logic to demonstrate the futility of using logic. The anti-intellectuals construct intricate intellectual arguments to prove the insufficiency of the intellect. Those who deny the competence of words to express thought use words in their denials. The proponents of poetry, myth, metaphor, and analogy argue for their theories by using literal prose, whose competence – even whose possibility – they deny. The anti-theologians use the revealed Word of God to show that there can be no revealed Word of God – or that if there could, it would remain impenetrable darkness and Mystery to our finite minds.

Nonsense Has Come

Is it any wonder that the world is grasping at straws – the straws of experientialism, mysticism, and drugs? After all, if people are told that the Bible contains insoluble mysteries, then is not a flight into mysticism to be expected? On what grounds can it be condemned? Certainly not on logical grounds or Biblical grounds, if logic is futile and the Bible unknowable. Moreover, if it cannot be condemned on logical or Biblical grounds, it cannot be condemned at all. If people are going to have a religion of the mysterious, they will not adopt Christianity: They will have a genuine mystery religion. The popularity of mysticism, drugs, and religious experience is the logical consequence of the irrationalism of the present age. There can and will be no Christian reformation – and no restoration of a free society – unless and until the irrationalism of the age is totally repudiated by Christians.

The Church Defenseless

Yet how shall they do it? The official spokesmen for Christianity have been fatally infected with irrationalism. The seminaries, which annually train thousands of men to teach millions of Christians, are the finishing schools of irrationalism, completing the job begun by the government schools and colleges. Most of the pulpits of the conservative churches (we are not speaking of the obviously-apostate churches) are occupied by graduates of the anti-theological schools. These products of modern anti-theological education, when asked to give a reason for the hope that is in them, can generally respond with only the intellectual analogue of a shrug – a mumble about Mystery. They have not grasped – and therefore cannot teach those for whom they are responsible – the first truth: "And you shall know the truth." Many, in fact, explicitly contradict Christ, saying that, at best, we possess only "pointers" to the truth, or something "similar" to the truth, a mere analogy. Is the impotence of the Christian church a puzzle? Is the fascination with pentecostalism, faith healing, Eastern Orthodoxy, and Roman Catholicism – all sensate and anti-intellectual religions – among members of Christian churches an enigma? Not when one understands the pious nonsense that is purveyed in the name of God in the religious colleges and seminaries.

The Trinity Foundation

The creators of The Trinity Foundation firmly believe that theology is too important to be left to the licensed theologians – the graduates of the schools of theology. They have created The Trinity Foundation for the express purpose of teaching the faithful all that the Scriptures contain – not warmed over, baptized,

Antichristian philosophies. Each member of the board of directors of The Trinity Foundation has signed this oath: "I believe that the Bible alone and the Bible in its entirety is the Word of God and, therefore, inerrant in the autographs. I believe that the system of truth presented in the Bible is best summarized in the *Westminster Confession of Faith.* So help me God."

The ministry of The Trinity Foundation is the presentation of the system of truth taught in Scripture as clearly and as completely as possible. We do not regard obscurity as a virtue, nor confusion as a sign of spirituality. Confusion, like all error, is sin, and teaching that confusion is all that Christians can hope for is doubly sin.

The presentation of the truth of Scripture necessarily involves the rejection of error. The Foundation has exposed and will continue to expose the irrationalism of the present age, whether its current spokesman be an existentialist philosopher or a professed Reformed theologian. We oppose anti-intellectualism, whether it be espoused by a Neo-orthodox theologian or a fundamentalist evangelist. We reject misology, whether it be on the lips of a Neo-evangelical or those of a Roman Catholic Charismatic. We repudiate agnosticism, whether it be secular or religious. To each error we bring the brilliant light of Scripture, proving all things, and holding fast to that which is true.

The Primacy of Theory

The ministry of The Trinity Foundation is not a "practical" ministry. If you are a pastor, we will not enlighten you on how to organize an ecumenical prayer meeting in your community or how to double church attendance in a year. If you are a homemaker, you will have to read elsewhere to find out how to become a total woman. If you are a businessman, we will not tell you how to develop a social conscience. The professing church is drowning in such "practical" advice.

The Trinity Foundation is unapologetically theoretical in its outlook, believing that theory without practice is dead, and that practice without theory is blind. The trouble with the professing church is not primarily in its practice, but in its theory. Church-goers and teachers do not know, and many do not even care to know, the doctrines of Scripture. Doctrine is intellectual, and churchgoers and teachers are generally anti-intellectual. Doctrine is ivory tower philosophy, and they scorn ivory towers. The ivory tower, however, is the control tower of a civilization. It is a fundamental, theoretical mistake of the "practical" men to think that they can be merely practical, for practice is always the practice of some theory. The relationship between theory and practice is the relationship between cause and effect. If a person believes correct theory, his practice will tend to be correct. The practice of contemporary Christians is immoral because it is the practice of false theories. It is a major theoretical mistake of the practical men to think that they can ignore the ivory towers of the philosophers and theologians as irrelevant to their lives. Every action that "practical" men take is governed by the thinking that has occurred in some ivory tower – whether that tower be the British Museum; the Academy; a home in Basel, Switzerland; or a tent in Israel.

In Understanding Be Men

It is the first duty of the Christian to understand correct theory – correct doctrine – and thereby implement correct practice. This order – first theory, then practice – is both logical and Biblical. It is, for example, exhibited in Paul's *Epistle to the Romans,* in which he spends the first eleven chapters expounding theory and the last five discussing practice. The contemporary teachers of Christians have not only reversed the Biblical order, they have inverted the Pauline emphasis on theory and practice. The virtually complete failure of the teachers of the professing church to instruct believers in correct doctrine is the cause of the misconduct and spiritual and cultural impotence of Christians. The church's lack of power is the result of its lack of truth. The *Gospel* is the power of God, not religious experiences or personal relationships. The church has no power because it has abandoned the Gospel, the good news, for a religion of experientialism. Twentieth-first-century American Christians are children carried about by every wind of doctrine, not knowing what they believe, or even if they believe anything for certain.

The chief purpose of The Trinity Foundation is to counteract the irrationalism of the age and to expose the errors of the teachers of the church. Our emphasis – on the Bible as the sole source of knowledge, on the primacy of truth, on the supreme importance of correct doctrine, and on the necessity for systematic and logical thinking – is almost unique in Christendom. To the extent that the church survives – and she will survive and flourish – it will be because of her increasing acceptance of these basic ideas and their logical implications.

We believe that The Trinity Foundation is filling a vacuum in Christendom. We are saying that Christianity is intellectually defensible – that, in fact, it is the only intellectually defensible system of thought. We are saying that God has made the wisdom of this world – whether that wisdom be called science, religion, philosophy, or common sense – foolishness. We are appealing to all Christians who have not conceded defeat in the intellectual battle with the world to join us in our efforts to raise a standard to which all men of sound mind can repair.

The love of truth, of God's Word, has all but disappeared in our time. We are committed to and pray for a great instauration. But though we may not see this reformation in our lifetimes, we believe it is our duty to present the whole counsel of God, because Christ has commanded it. The results of our teaching are in God's hands, not ours. Whatever those results, his Word is never taught in vain, but always accomplishes the result that he intended it to accomplish. Professor Gordon H. Clark has stated our view well:

> There have been times in the history of God's people, for example, in the days of Jeremiah, when refreshing grace and widespread revival were not to be expected: The time was one of chastisement. If this twentieth century is of a similar nature, individual Christians here and there can find comfort and strength in a study of God's Word. But if God has decreed happier days for us, and if we may expect a world-shaking and genuine spiritual awakening, then it is the author's belief that a zeal for souls, however necessary, is not the sufficient condition. Have there not been devout saints in every age, numerous enough to carry on a revival? Twelve such persons are plenty. What distinguishes the arid ages from the period of the Reformation, when nations were moved as they had not been since Paul preached in Ephesus, Corinth, and Rome, is the latter's fullness of knowledge of God's Word. To echo an early Reformation thought, when the ploughman and the garage attendant know the Bible as well as the theologian does, and know it better than some contemporary theologians, then the desired awakening shall have already occurred.

In addition to publishing books, the Foundation publishes a monthly newsletter, *The Trinity Review.* Subscriptions to *The*

Review are free to U.S. addresses; please write to the address on the order form to become a subscriber. If you would like further information or would like to join us in our work, please let us know.

The Trinity Foundation is a non-profit foundation, tax exempt under section 501 (c)(3) of the Internal Revenue Code of 1954. You can help us disseminate the Word of God through your tax-deductible contributions to the Foundation.

JOHN W. ROBBINS

Intellectual Ammunition

T HE Trinity Foundation is committed to bringing every philosophical and theological thought captive to Christ. The
books listed below are designed to accomplish that goal. They
are written with two subordinate purposes: (1) to demolish all
non-Christian claims to knowledge; and (2) to build a system of
truth based upon the Bible alone.

PHILOSOPHY

Ancient Philosophy
Gordon H. Clark   Trade paperback $24.95
This book covers the thousand years from the Pre-
Socratics to Plotinus. It represents some of the early work
of Dr. Clark – the work that made his academic reputa-
tion. It is an excellent college text.

Behaviorism and Christianity
Gordon H. Clark   Trade paperback $5.95
Behaviorism is a critique of both secular and religious
behaviorists. It includes chapters on John Watson, Edgar
S. Singer, Jr., Gilbert Ryle, B. F. Skinner, and Donald
MacKay. Clark's refutation of behaviorism and his argu-
ment for a Christian doctrine of man are unanswerable.

A Christian Philosophy of Education   Hardback $18.95
Gordon H. Clark   Trade paperback $12.95
    The first edition of this book was published in 1946. It sparked the contemporary interest in Christian schools. In the 1970s, Dr. Clark thoroughly revised and updated it, and it is needed now more than ever. Its chapters include: The Need for a World-View; The Christian World-View; The Alternative to Christian Theism; Neutrality; Ethics; The Christian Philosophy of Education; Academic Matters; and Kindergarten to University. Three appendices are included: The Relationship of Public Education to Christianity; A Protestant World-View; and Art and the Gospel.

A Christian View of Men and Things   Hardback $29.95
Gordon H. Clark   Trade paperback $14.95
    No other book achieves what *A Christian View* does: the presentation of Christianity as it applies to history, politics, ethics, science, religion, and epistemology. Dr. Clark's command of both worldly philosophy and Scripture is evident on every page, and the result is a breathtaking and invigorating challenge to the wisdom of this world.

Clark Speaks from the Grave
Gordon H. Clark   Trade paperback $3.95
    Dr. Clark chides some of his critics for their failure to defend Christianity competently. *Clark Speaks* is a stimulating and illuminating discussion of the errors of contemporary apologists.

Ecclesiastical Megalomania:
The Economic and Political Thought
of the Roman Catholic Church   Hardback $29.95
John W. Robbins   Trade paperback $19.95
     This detailed and thorough analysis and critique of the
social teaching of the Roman Church-State is the only such
book available by a Christian economist and political philosopher. The book's conclusions reveal the Roman Church-
State to be an advocate of its own brand of global religious
Fascism. *Ecclesiastical Megalomania* includes the complete
text of the *Donation of Constantine* and Lorenzo Valla's
exposé of the hoax.

Education, Christianity, and the State
J. Gresham Machen   Trade paperback $9.95
     Machen was one of the foremost educators, theologians,
and defenders of Christianity in the twentieth century. The
author of several scholarly books, Machen saw clearly that
if Christianity is to survive and flourish, a system of Christian schools must be established. This collection of essays
and speeches captures his thoughts on education over nearly
three decades.

Essays on Ethics and Politics
Gordon H. Clark   Trade paperback $10.95
     Dr. Clark's essays, written over the course of five decades,
are a major statement of Christian ethics.

Gordon H. Clark: Personal Recollections
John W. Robbins, editor   Trade paperback $6.95
     Friends of Dr. Clark have written their recollections of

the man. Contributors include family members, colleagues, students, and friends such as Harold Lindsell, Carl Henry, Ronald Nash, and Anna Marie Hager.

Historiography: Secular and Religious
Gordon H. Clark   Trade paperback $13.95
   In this masterful work, Dr. Clark applies his philosophy to the writing of history, examining all the major schools of historiography.

An Introduction to Christian Philosophy
Gordon H. Clark   Trade paperback $8.95
   In 1966 Dr. Clark delivered three lectures on philosophy at Wheaton College. In these lectures he criticizes secular philosophy and launches a philosophical revolution in the name of Christ.

Language and Theology
Gordon H. Clark   Trade paperback $9.95
   There are two main currents in twentieth-century philosophy – language philosophy and existentialism. Both are hostile to Christianity. Dr. Clark disposes of language philosophy in this brilliant critique of Bertrand Russell, Ludwig Wittgenstein, Rudolf Carnap, A. J. Ayer, Langdon Gilkey, and many others.

Logic   Hardback $16.95
Gordon H. Clark   Trade paperback $10.95
   Written as a textbook for Christian schools, *Logic* is another unique book from Dr. Clark's pen. His presentation of the laws of thought, which must be followed if Scrip-

ture is to be understood correctly, and which are found in Scripture itself, is both clear and thorough. *Logic* is an indispensable book for the thinking Christian.

Logic Workbook
Elihu Carranza   Oversize paperback $11.95
  Designed to be used in conjunction with Dr. Clark's textbook *Logic,* this *Workbook* contains hundreds of exercises and test questions on perforated pages for ease of use by students.

Lord God of Truth, Concerning the Teacher
Gordon H. Clark and Aurelius Augustine
                                          Trade paperback $7.95
  This essay by Dr. Clark summarizes many of the most telling arguments against empiricism and defends the Biblical teaching that we know God and truth immediately. The dialogue by Augustine is a refutation of empirical language philosophy.

The Philosophy of Science and Belief in God
Gordon H. Clark   Trade paperback $8.95
  In opposing the contemporary idolatry of science, Dr. Clark analyzes three major aspects of science: the problem of motion, Newtonian science, and modern theories of physics. His conclusion is that science, while it may be useful, is always false; and he demonstrates its falsity in numerous ways. Since science is always false, it can offer no alternative to the Bible and Christianity.

Religion, Reason and Revelation
Gordon H. Clark   Trade paperback $10.95
   One of Dr. Clark's apologetical masterpieces, *Religion, Reason and Revelation* has been praised for the clarity of its thought and language. It includes these chapters: Is Christianity a Religion? Faith and Reason; Inspiration and Language; Revelation and Morality; and God and Evil. It is must reading for all serious Christians.

The Scripturalism of Gordon H. Clark
W. Gary Crampton   Trade paperback $9.95
   Dr. Crampton has written an introduction to the philosophy of Gordon H. Clark that is helpful to both beginners and advanced students of theology. This book includes a bibliography of Dr. Clark's works.

Thales to Dewey:
A History of Philosophy   Hardback $29.95
Gordon H. Clark   Trade paperback $21.95
   This is the best one-volume history of philosophy in print.

Three Types of Religious Philosophy
Gordon H. Clark   Trade paperback $6.95
   In this book on apologetics, Dr. Clark examines empiricism, rationalism, dogmatism, and contemporary irrationalism, which does not rise to the level of philosophy. He offers an answer to the question, "How can Christianity be defended before the world?"

William James and John Dewey
Gordon H. Clark   Trade paperback $8.95
William James and John Dewey are two of the most influential philosophers America has produced. Their philosophies of instrumentalism and pragmatism are hostile
to Christianity, and Dr. Clark demolishes their arguments.

Without a Prayer: Ayn Rand and the Close of Her System
John W. Robbins   Hardback $27.95
Ayn Rand has been a best-selling author since 1957. *Without a Prayer* discusses Objectivism's epistemology, theology, ethics, and politics in detail. Appendices include analyses of books by Leonard Peikoff and David Kelley, as well
as several essays on Christianity and philosophy.

THEOLOGY

Against the Churches: The Trinity Review 1989-1998
John W. Robbins, editor   Oversize hardback $39.95
This is the second volume of essays from *The Trinity Re-
view*, covering its second ten years, from 1989-1998. This
volume, like the first, is fully indexed and is very useful in
research and in the classroom. Authors include: Gordon
Clark, John Robbins, Peter Herz, Gary Crampton, Charles
Hodge, Joel Parkinson, J. C. Ryle, Horatius Bonar, Robert
L. Dabney, and Godwell Chan.

Against the World: The Trinity Review 1978-1988
John W. Robbins, editor   Oversize hardback $34.95
This is a clothbound collection of the essays published in
The Trinity Review from 1978 to 1988, 70 in all. It is a valu-
able source of information and arguments explaining and
defending Christianity.

The Atonement

Gordon H. Clark   Trade paperback $8.95

In *The Atonement,* Dr. Clark discusses the covenants, the virgin birth and incarnation, federal headship and representation, the relationship between God's sovereignty and justice, and much more. He analyzes traditional views of the atonement and criticizes them in the light of Scripture alone.

The Biblical Doctrine of Man

Gordon H. Clark   Trade paperback $6.95

Is man soul and body or soul, spirit, and body? What is the image of God? Is Adam's sin imputed to his children? Is evolution true? Are men totally depraved? What is the heart? These are some of the questions discussed and answered from Scripture in this book.

By Scripture Alone

W Gary Crampton   Trade paperback $12.95

This is a clear and thorough explanation of the Scriptural doctrine of Scripture and a refutation of the recent Romanist attack on the Scripture as the Word of God

The Changing of the Guard

Mark W. Karlberg   Trade paperback $3.95

This essay is a critical discussion of Westminster Seminary's anti-Reformational and un-Biblical teaching on the doctrine of justification. Dr. Karlberg exposes the doctrine of justification by faith and works – not *sola fide* – taught at Westminster Seminary for the past 25 years, by Professors Norman Shepherd, Richard Gaffin, John Frame, and others.

The Church Effeminate

John W. Robbins, editor   Hardback $29.95

This is a collection of 39 essays by the best theologians of the church on the doctrine of the church: Martin Luther, John Calvin, Benjamin Warfield, Gordon Clark, J. C. Ryle, and many more. The essays cover the structure, function, and purpose of the church.

The Clark-Van Til Controversy

Herman Hoeksema   Trade paperback $7.95

This collection of essays by the founder of the Protestant Reformed Churches – essays written at the time of the Clark-Van Til controversy in the 1940s – is one of the best commentaries on those events in print.

Cornelius Van Til: The Man and The Myth

John W. Robbins   Trade paperback $2.45

The actual teachings of this eminent Philadelphia theologian have been obscured by the myths that surround him. This book penetrates those myths and criticizes Van Til's surprisingly unorthodox views of God and the Bible.

The Everlasting Righteousness

Horatius Bonar   Trade paperback $8.95

Originally published in 1874, the language of Bonar's masterpiece on justification by faith alone has been updated and Americanized for easy reading and clear understanding. This is one of the best books ever written on justification.

Faith and Saving Faith
Gordon H. Clark   Trade paperback $6.95
    The views of the Roman Catholic Church, John Calvin,
Thomas Manton, John Owen, Charles Hodge, and B. B.
Warfield are discussed in this book. Is the object of faith a
person or a proposition? Is faith more than belief? Is belief
thinking with assent, as Augustine said? In a world chaotic
with differing views of faith, Dr. Clark clearly explains the
Biblical view of faith and saving faith.

God and Evil: The Problem Solved
Gordon H. Clark   Trade paperback $4.95
    This volume is Chapter 5 of *Religion, Reason and Revela-
tion,* in which Dr. Clark presents his solution to the problem of evil.

God-Breathed: The Divine Inspiration of the Bible
Louis Gaussen   Trade paperback $16.95
    Gaussen, a nineteenth-century Swiss Reformed pastor,
collected the hundreds of passages in which the Bible claims
to be the Word of God. This is a massive defense of the
doctrine of the plenary and verbal inspiration of Scripture.

God's Hammer: The Bible and Its Critics
Gordon H. Clark   Trade paperback $10.95
    The starting point of Christianity, the doctrine on which
all other doctrines depend, is "The Bible alone, and the
Bible in its entirety, is the Word of God written, and, therefore, inerrant in the autographs." Over the centuries the
opponents of Christianity, with Satanic shrewdness, have
concentrated their attacks on the truthfulness and com-

pleteness of the Bible. In the twentieth century the attack was not so much in the fields of history and archaeology as in philosophy. Dr. Clark's brilliant defense of the complete truthfulness of the Bible is captured in this collection of eleven major essays.

The Holy Spirit

Gordon H. Clark   Trade paperback $8.95

This discussion of the third person of the Trinity is both concise and exact. Dr. Clark includes chapters on the work of the Spirit, sanctification, and Pentecostalism. This book is part of his multi-volume systematic theology that began appearing in print in 1985.

The Incarnation

Gordon H. Clark   Trade paperback $8.95

Who is Christ? The attack on the doctrine of the incarnation in the nineteenth and twentieth centuries has been vigorous, but the orthodox response has been lame. Dr. Clark reconstructs the doctrine of the incarnation, building and improving upon the Chalcedonian definition.

The Johannine Logos

Gordon H. Clark   Trade paperback $5.95

Dr. Clark analyzes the relationship between Christ, who is the truth, and the Bible. He explains why John used the same word to refer to both Christ and his teaching. Chapters deal with the Prologue to John's Gospel; *Logos* and *Rheemata;* Truth; and Saving Faith.

Justification by Faith Alone
Charles Hodge   Trade paperback $10.95
    Charles Hodge of Princeton Seminary was the best American theologian of the nineteenth century. Here, for the first time, are his two major essays on justification in one volume. This book is essential in defending the faith.

Karl Barth's Theological Method
Gordon H. Clark   Trade paperback $18.95
    Karl Barth's Theological Method is perhaps the best critique of the Neo-orthodox theologian Karl Barth ever written. Dr. Clark discusses Barth's view of revelation, language, and Scripture, focusing on his method of writing theology, rather than presenting a comprehensive analysis of the details of Barth's theology.

Logical Criticisms of Textual Criticism
Gordon H. Clark   Trade paperback $3.25
    Dr. Clark's acute mind enables him to demonstrate the inconsistencies, assumptions, and flights of fancy that characterize the science of New Testament criticism.

New Testament Greek for Beginners   Hardback $16.95
J. Gresham Machen   Trade paperback $10.95
    Long a standard text, *New Testament Greek for Beginners* is extremely helpful in the study of the New Testament in the original Greek. It may profitably be used by high school, college, and seminary students, either in a classroom setting or in self-study. Machen was Professor of New Testament Literature and Exegesis at Princeton Theological Seminary and the founder of Westminster

Theological Seminary and the Orthodox Presbyterian Church.

Predestination

Gordon H. Clark   Trade paperback $10.95

Dr. Clark thoroughly discusses one of the most controversial and pervasive doctrines of the Bible: that God is, quite literally, Almighty. Free will, the origin of evil, God's omniscience, creation, and the new birth are all presented within a Scriptural framework. The objections of those who do not believe in Almighty God are considered and refuted. This edition also contains the text of the booklet, *Predestination in the Old Testament.*

Sanctification

Gordon H. Clark   Trade paperback $8.95

In this book, which is part of Dr. Clark's multi-volume systematic theology, he discusses historical theories of sanctification, the sacraments, and the Biblical doctrine of sanctification.

Study Guide to the Westminster Confession

W. Gary Crampton   Oversize paperback $10.95

This *Study Guide* may be used by individuals or classes. It contains a paragraph-by-paragraph summary of the *Westminster Confession,* and questions for the student to answer. Space for answers is provided. The *Guide* will be most beneficial when used in conjunction with Dr. Clark's *What Do Presbyterians Believe?*

A Theology of the Holy Spirit
Frederick Dale Bruner   Trade paperback, $16.95
    First published in 1970, this book has been hailed by
reviewers as "thorough," "fair," "comprehensive," "devastating," "the most significant book on the Holy Spirit,"
and "scholarly." Gordon Clark described this book in his
own book *The Holy Spirit* as "a masterly and exceedingly
well researched exposition of Pentecostalism. The docu-
mentation is superb, as is also his penetrating analysis of
their non-scriptural and sometimes contradictory conclusions."

The Trinity
Gordon H. Clark   Trade paperback $8.95
    Apart from the doctrine of Scripture, no teaching of the
Bible is more fundamental than the doctrine of God. Dr.
Clark's defense of the orthodox doctrine of the Trinity is a
principal portion of his systematic theology. There are
chapters on the Deity of Christ; Augustine; the Incompre-
hensibility of God; Bavinck and Van Til; and the Holy
Spirit; among others.

What Calvin Says
W. Gary Crampton   Trade paperback $8.95
    This is a clear, readable, and thorough introduction to
the theology of John Calvin.

What Do Presbyterians Believe?
Gordon H. Clark   Trade paperback $10.95
    This classic is the best commentary on the *Westminster
Confession of Faith* ever written.

CLARK'S COMMENTARIES
ON THE NEW TESTAMENT

Colossians	Trade paperback	$6.95
Ephesians	Trade paperback	$8.95
First Corinthians	Trade paperback	$10.95
First John	Trade paperback	$10.95
First and Second Thessalonians	Trade paperback	$5.95
New Heavens, New Earth (*First* and *Second Peter*)	Trade paperback	$10.95
The Pastoral Epistles (1 and 2 *Timothy* and *Titus*)	Hardback	$29.95
	Trade paperback	$14.95
Philippians	Trade paperback	$9.95

All of Clark's commentaries are expository, not technical, and are written for the Christian layman. His purpose is to explain the text clearly and accurately so that the Word of God will be thoroughly known by every Christian.

The Trinity Library

We will send you one copy of each of the 58 books listed above for $500 (retail value nearly $800), postpaid to any address in the U.S. You may also order the books you want individually on the order form on the next page. Because some of the books are in short supply, we must reserve the right to substitute others of equal or greater value in The Trinity Library. This special offer expires October 31, 2005.

Order Form

NAME _____

ADDRESS _____

_____

TELEPHONE _____

E-MAIL _____

Please:

❑ add my name to the mailing list for *The Trinity Review*. I understand that there is no charge for single copies of *The Review* sent to a U.S. address.

❑ accept my tax deductible contribution of U.S. $ _____ .

❑ send me ____ copies of *By Scripture Alone*. I enclose as payment U.S. $ _____.

❑ send me the Trinity Library of 58 books. I enclose U.S. $500 as full payment.

❑ send me the following books. I enclose full payment in the amount of U.S. $ _____ for them.

_____

_____

_____

_____

The Trinity Foundation
Post Office Box 68
Unicoi, Tennessee 37692
Website: http://www.trinityfoundation.org/
United States of America

Shipping: Please add $5.00 for the first book, and 50 cents for each additional book. For foreign orders, please add $6.00 for the first book and $1.00 for each additional book.